SOCIAL ANXIETY RELIEF GUIDE FOR TEENAGE GIRLS

HOW TO REWIRE THE BRAIN FROM INSECURE AND SELF-CONSCIOUS TO BRAVE AND EMPOWERED

PAGET KAGY

CONTENTS

A GIFT TO OUR READERS

EMPOWER . EXPAND . INSPIRE

We would love to gift our readers with the "5 Daily Rules for Empowerment Guide" and cheatsheet.

Click below and let us know where to deliver it to:
http://www.EmpowerInspireExpand.com

INTRODUCTION

When I was fourteen, my mother gifted me a self-help book (with the best intentions) because she sensed that something was very wrong. I was reclusive and unresponsive, and I didn't want to talk to my parents about what I was going through at school. Suffice to say, after reading the first few pages of the book, I stashed it away on my bookshelf (hid it in a drawer), and never opened it again. I wasn't interested in reading a clinical psychologist's thoughts on what I was going through as a teenager.

I didn't need more exercises telling me to close my eyes and breathe, and everything would feel better. I wanted someone to speak to me and give me a reason to do the exercises in the first place. I wanted to know that they would actually help me.

I don't want *this* book to be *that* book for you.

I know how you feel. I've been there. That sinking pit in your stomach as you go to class—the nervousness about the future and what it will hold. The judgmental eyes of peers leering at you from different corners of the hallway.

Sometimes you feel lost. Inadequate. Maybe even invisible.

Growing up, I had it a little tougher than most. As one of the only Asian Americans in a predominantly Caucasian area, I stood out like a sore thumb. The fact that I had a little extra puppy fat and some serious acne didn't help, either. People shouted slurs at me in class, and I found myself the center of many colorful jokes. To make matters worse, I was a shy introvert who could barely deliver a book report without my voice shaking. It wasn't a fun experience.

In retrospect, my self-esteem was pretty much non-existent. But you wouldn't know that just by looking at me. My behavior was "normal," I got good grades, wasn't a trouble-maker, and had supportive parents. However, I was too scared to tell them about the ridicule I was suffering in school because I didn't want them to be ashamed of me. I wanted them to see me as the strong, cool, confident kid everyone liked and admired. Not the self-conscious girl who secretly felt uncool whenever she walked through the quad. At one point, I remember catching my reflection in a car window, thinking, "why can't I be pretty like the other girls in my class? Why do I feel so *different*?"

I always felt like the sidekick in my own life and never the main character. Even though I knew I had more to share with the world, something was holding me back from doing it, and that thing would continue to hold me back until my late twenties, until I finally decided to examine myself on a deeper level.

I say all this now because I know that *many* teens suffer from the feelings I did, but they're too afraid to admit it or don't know how to express it. According to the National Institute of Health, nearly one in three teenagers suffers from some form of anxiety disorder. You may have unique challenges and reasons for feeling the way you do, but you aren't alone. And you *are* strong enough to overcome them.

I believe the magnitude of the challenges we face in life is directly proportional to how empowered we can become. After all, some of the greatest superhero movies are based on protagonists with the most dramatic transformations (think: *Spiderman, Superman, Captain America*). We love to watch the main character evolve from the disempowered outcast to the triumphant hero by the film's end. While actual timelines are a little longer than a two-and-a-half-hour movie, that same journey is in you, too.

There were times in my teenage years and throughout my early twenties when I felt so disempowered that I could barely get out of bed in the morning. I went through the motions of waiting for things to change but feeling hopeless that they never would. I became a passive observer of my life instead of an active participant. *"When is this going to end?"* I thought.

Cut to over fifteen years later, and things turned out okay— more than okay. I have a great network of friends, love what I do, and most importantly, I see myself as the hero of my life. The road on your journey may not always be easy, but the longer you wait to address the issues that cause you pain, the harder it becomes to heal them. That's why I'm going to share with you some strategies, perspectives, and exercises I wish I had when I was battling my anxiety as a teen.

It would have been helpful to know that I wasn't alone in my feeling alone–that embracing my vulnerabilities would have made me stronger, not weaker, and that a bit of self-reflection would go a long way.

Now you might be wondering if you're even suffering from anxiety in the first place. "Is it *that* bad?" is a common thought. Most people DO suffer from some level of anxiety; it's just a matter of how much and whether it negatively impacts their everyday lives. If you relate to more than one of the following statements, you can benefit from the tools in this book:

- I often second guess my decisions and worry about what others think of me.
- I often worry about the outlook of my future.
- I have trouble saying "no" to people around me because I'm afraid they won't like me.

- When something doesn't go my way, I often blame myself for not being good enough.
- I often assume people are judging me negatively.
- I often think that other people are better than me.
- I have trouble seeing my value and unique gifts and talents.
- My lack of confidence prevents me from doing things I would otherwise like to do.
- I assume that other people won't accept me.
- I tend to expect the worst outcome of a situation.

In this book, you'll discover practical, non-clinical exercises to help you deal with those feelings of anxiety and train your reactive brain into a more rational and positive one. I'll share real stories from my teenage years, provide helpful perspectives on what you might be going through and demonstrate how you can turn emotional triggers into positive learning experiences.

Most importantly, I want you to define your own hero's journey. I want you to step into your power as the main character of your life and stop feeling like the sidekick.

There will always be another obstacle, another failure, and another stumble. Whether that applies to your grades, relationships, or family, the critical factor determining your success in life is your ability to meet those challenges head-on and have the tools in your back pocket to face them proactively.

I won't promise that this book will make everything a breeze. But I promise you this: if you dedicate time to develop your internal strength now, every challenge you face in the future will not only make you stronger, but at some point, you'll walk around with the knowledge of how truly powerful you are. Here's a little secret: that power is already inside of you right now. It's just waiting to be unlocked, and you're the person holding the key.

I guarantee that some of the exercises in this book you're not going to like. They're going to feel "stupid" or "lame." But take it from someone who didn't have tools until much later in life–get a head start now, and your future self will thank you.

Are you ready to confront the negative thoughts in your head, step outside your comfort zone, and become the hero of your life? Let's get started.

THE BRAIN WIRED

HOW YOUR BRAIN WORKS IN A NUTSHELL

> *"The human brain starts working the moment you are born and never stops until you stand up to speak in public."*

> — *GEORGE JESSEL*

First, let's take a quick look at how your brain works regarding your logical and emotional mind.

It's helpful to have a general understanding of the mechanics of the brain because it can show us how unnecessary and, quite frankly, ridiculous a lot of our thoughts are.

In the simplest terms, the brain breaks up into three major centers--the amygdala (emotional brain), the pre-frontal cortex (smart brain), and the brain stem (survival brain). The amygdala (emotional brain) is for storing and sorting emotions and memories. For example, when you accidentally leaned on the stove and burned your elbow? It will store that memory to save you a burned arm (or worse) in the future.

The pre-frontal cortex (smart brain) helps you solve problems, like when you take a math test or write a history paper. This part of your brain deals with logic and information. It can command your amygdala (emotional brain) to beware of perceived danger. Thankfully, it can also calm your emotional brain down when that threat proves to be harmless.

Lastly, the brain stem (survival brain) is responsible for your body's functions that you never have to think about, like breathing, maintaining your heart rate, and circulating your blood. This part of the brain is also responsible for your fight, flight, or freeze response when the amygdala (emotional brain) senses impending danger.

It's a beautiful system that worked perfectly during caveman days when we were sizing up a potential mate, sheltering our young from harm, and facing potential danger around every corner. But for the modern-day life of social media feeds, peer pressure, and school stress? It tends to trip us up and make our lives feel like war zones.

For example, let's say your crush walks into the room right before you're about to give a presentation. Instead of your smart brain carrying on with the presentation, your amygdala (emotional brain) kicks into overdrive and tries to warn you of impending danger (looking stupid). It then signals your brain stem (survival brain) to activate the fight, flight, or freeze response. Your mouth dries up, you choke on your words, and your brain suddenly forgets everything you scripted the night before. And there you have it, the brain at its worst.

Even when we receive a disappointing text or see an embarrassing social media post, our survival brain can bring us into a state of physical panic. Our heart rates increase, our palms sweat, and that sinking feeling in the pit of our stomach leads us to impulsively text the first thing that comes to our minds. Have you ever sent a text you immediately wished you could take back? Yeah, that's your emotional and survival brain at its best.

Of course, this system is great if we're hiking in the woods and a bear crosses our path. But unfortunately, our brains can't tell the difference between a life-threatening physical danger and a harmless, heightened emotion caused by the latest gossip.

Therefore, part of the practice we'll have to cultivate in taming our anxiety will be recognizing when the emotional brain is taking over so we can activate our smart brains instead.

SELF-AWARENESS

THE MAGIC KEY TO UNLOCKING ALL GROWTH

> *"Until you make the unconscious conscious, it will direct your life, and you will call it fate."*
>
> — *CARL JUNG*

If there is one thing that I want you to remember from this chapter, it's this: self-awareness is the key to all growth.

A sprinter doesn't get faster because she refuses to train, a ballerina doesn't become more precise because she neglects her poor form, and a cook doesn't become world-class by ignoring honest feedback. Likewise, you can't become the best version of yourself if you don't first and foremost know yourself—the good, the bad, and the ugly.

Deep self-awareness is beyond knowing that your socks don't match or that you have food stuck in your teeth. True self-awareness is the practice of honestly and objectively observing your feelings, thoughts, opinions, behaviors, and actions from a place of total objectivity.

At an even higher level, it's asking questions about what you're observing: "Why *do* I always assume the worst will happen? Why *am* I always getting down on myself? Why *does* that comment make me mad?"

First, let me make a distinction between self-consciousness, which focuses on other people's perceptions of you, and self-awareness, which focuses on your inside perception of yourself.

I lacked self-awareness when I was a teen, but I had plenty of self-consciousness. I was self-conscious about my clothes, looks, backpack, and smile. In fact, I was so preoccupied with what other people thought about me, I didn't even have room in my brain to consider what I thought about myself. This pervading self-consciousness and lack of self-awareness only resulted in a secret longing to "fit in" and feel accepted by my peers.

My need for acceptance was so extreme that when I was 14, I asked my mom to take me to this trendy clothing store to buy the latest pair of jeans all the popular girls wore. I smiled giddily as I took the jeans off the rack. Then I saw the price tag. $250. Big gulp. As I slipped into each leg, I knew they were too tight for me, but I was so determined to get them that I didn't care. My mom urged me not to buy them because money was tight, but I was so fixated on the idea of fitting in that I walked back into the store and spent $250 on a pair of jeans that didn't fit.

If I had practiced self-awareness, I would have seen that buying that overpriced, ill-fitting pair of jeans was just an attempt to win acceptance from others because, deep down, I didn't accept myself. I would have realized that I was spending too much energy (and money) trying to get people to value me instead of seeing my own value. I would have understood that no one's approval would ever make up for what I lacked on the inside–a sense of self-worth.

With a bit of help from deep self-awareness, I would have been able to ask myself: "Why do I need other people to accept me so badly? What beliefs about myself make me feel like I need their approval? Do I really think my value hinges on a pair of jeans?"

Of course, at the time, I didn't have the tools of self-awareness to stop me from making bad choices, and unfortunately, in the years following that purchase, I would continue to seek quick fixes. I'm sure you've heard the Einstein quote: "Insanity is doing the same thing over and over again and expecting different results." Unsurprising, none of my superficial efforts led to a different result. Self-awareness would have saved me a lot of wasted time, energy, and frustration going around and around on a hamster wheel.

There's a cliché saying that people can only love you as much as you love yourself. As lame as that sounds, it's the truth. People will only respect you as much as you respect yourself, people will only value you as much as you value yourself, and so forth. I'm sure you get the picture. For years, I was looking for an external solution that would make me feel better in the moment instead of taking the time to understand the root cause of my suffering. I was forced to learn the hard way.

Just in case you were wondering, those same jeans now sell for $25 online. That's the thing about trends. They don't last. Your self-perception? That stays with you for the rest of your life.

So let's dig a little deeper into your own life. Are you aware of why you make the decisions you do? How well do you know yourself, and what motivates you? Can you take a step back from your everyday actions and analyze the thoughts behind them?

Here's a quick exercise to help you practice self-awareness.

EXERCISE

TRACK YOUR DECISIONS

Get out a pen and paper. I want you to catalog some of your choices in the past few days. They could be anything from "I got a sandwich for lunch instead of pizza," "I invited my friend over this weekend," or "I wore a pink t-shirt today." It doesn't matter what you write down, as long as you have a good list of about ten.

For example, a list might look something like this:

1. I had a lengthy text convo with a friend last night.
2. I went on a jog today.
3. I didn't raise my hand in class even though I wanted to.
4. I spent the car ride home on my phone and ignored my mom.
5. I skipped breakfast today.
6. I gave my friend my homework to copy.
7. I posted a selfie at the mall.
8. I spent four hours on homework.
9. I spent an hour on social media.
10. I stayed at home instead of hanging out with friends.

Then I want you to write down WHY you made that choice. Be honest, and dig as deep as possible. Taking a moment to ask ourselves WHY we do the things we do, even the most minor things, can help us develop the critical self-awareness that there is a reason behind every choice we make. Knowing these reasons and seeing patterns in them can give us so much insight into what motivates our actions, and more importantly, *why*.

Some are going to be easier than others, but here's an example of what that might look like:

1. I had a lengthy text convo with a friend last night… because I was trying to avoid doing homework… because it was hard, and I didn't want to put in the effort.
2. I went on a jog today…because I overate the day before and I don't want to gain weight…because if I gain weight, I won't be pretty and people won't like me.
3. I didn't raise my hand in class…because even though I wanted to, I thought I'd look stupid to other people…and if I looked stupid to others, I could be made fun of. It was easier to lay low.
4. I spent the car ride home on my phone…because I wanted to avoid talking to my mom…because she would judge me about my grades, and it would make me feel bad.
5. I skipped breakfast today even though I was hungry…because I didn't want to feel bloated in class…because people would think I looked fat.

6. I gave my friend my homework…because I feel like she will be mad at me if I don't and she won't be my friend anymore.

7. I posted a selfie at the mall…because I wanted to show my classmates that I was having fun…because I want them to think that I'm cool.

8. I spent four hours on homework…because I slacked on yesterday's assignments and needed to make up for that today.

9. I spent an hour on social media…because I wanted to distract myself from thinking about a crappy text I received from a friend…because it doesn't make me feel good.

10. I stayed at home instead of hanging out with friends…because they invited another girl to hang out with them who doesn't like me…and I didn't want to feel uncomfortable.

When you read the list I wrote above, you can quickly see how many of our decisions in life are based on thoughts, beliefs, and assumptions that aren't necessarily true. And a whole lot of them are based on negative self-perceptions!

For example, let's take #7. Posting a selfie is something everyone does. There's nothing special or strange about the act in itself. But knowing why you are posting a selfie on social media is worth examining. Suppose you only post on social media to show others how "cool" you are. In that case, we would naturally explore the questions: "Why do I need to prove my "coolness" to other people? How much do I rely on other people's opinions of me to feel good about myself?"

Now, we are all guilty of sharing the highlighted versions of ourselves on social media, so I'm not advocating that you beat yourself up about it. However, it would be a good practice to recognize when you do it, so you can avoid placing too much importance on things that ultimately don't matter. Self-awareness gives you the ability to remind yourself of these facts!

When we fail to examine our actions beyond our narrow perspectives, we can lead ourselves down dangerous rabbit holes of thinking that may be abusive, unhealthy, and cause unnecessary anxiety. For instance, if we post something on social media in the hopes of looking "cool" but it doesn't get the number of likes or comments we want, we can quickly jump to some pretty negative conclusions like "I'm not cool enough," or "I feel embarrassed" or "No one likes me." When, in fact, nothing in your life has actually changed for the better or worse.

Using a little self-awareness in that example, you might feel disappointed by the outcome momentarily, but you can quickly move on to more important things in your life when you realize how inconsequential the situation really is.

Practicing self-awareness and noticing why you're motivated to do what you do is also an excellent tool for exploring how we can improve.

Let's take example #1 from the above list. We all procrastinate. Over a decade later, and I'm still guilty of procrastinating. But going a step further and asking why we procrastinate might give us helpful insight into the assumptions we have about ourselves that hold us back in life.

For example, suppose you are procrastinating because you find the work challenging, and doing it makes you feel bad about yourself. In that case, that's a good thing to know. Maybe understanding that your value is not determined by how easily you can do the homework will make the work less frustrating. If you view the challenge of homework as an opportunity to practice patience and resilience with yourself, you'll develop a valuable life skill that will serve you far beyond that one homework assignment.

Let me give an example of where I could have benefited from more self-awareness. In college, I decided to major in math because it was an easy subject for me in high school (not a good reason, as I soon found out). That is, until I took my first upper-division math class. I stared blankly at the professor as he rattled about concepts that went completely over my head. My peers raised their hands and nodded their heads thoughtfully while I sat there lost and confused.

My biggest problem? I wasn't used to being challenged in math, and for the first time, math made me feel like a "loser" compared to the other students in my class. Before the end of the week, I dropped out of the course.

Instead of buckling down, letting go of my pride, and getting assistance from a teacher's aide, I quit because I thought needing extra help meant I was "dumb" and, therefore, less worthy. I wasn't just running away from the hard work of the course. I was running away from the feelings of embarrassment for not being good enough. My pride couldn't handle the fact that maybe I'd have to work harder than my peers to understand what they picked up naturally.

Of course, the cruel irony is that I didn't end up escaping the lesson. The following semester, when I decided to switch my major to history, I found myself in one of the hardest history seminars in the whole field.

While classmates quoted the concepts of French philosopher Foucault like kindergarten nursery rhymes, I was flipping through the dictionary just to keep up. Yet again, I found myself the dunce of the class. Of course, my immediate impulse was to change seminars. I even went to my counselor's office and pleaded with her, but to no avail. I was forced to deal with the challenge this time. And boy, did it turn out to be a challenge.

At first, I did what any student in denial does—I procrastinated. I ended up with C's on my papers—even a D+. It wasn't long before I realized that I was at an impasse. I could continue to slack off and barely pass, or I could roll up my sleeves, step outside my comfort zone and admit that I needed extra help.

Halfway into the semester, I finally lost my pride and started applying myself. I had to accept that my peers were naturally more comfortable with the concepts than I was, and that didn't make me any less of a person. While they were writing papers in their sleep, I worked harder in that class than I ever have, and in the end, I earned a B.

If I had practiced deep self-awareness sooner, I could have seen that my pride was getting in the way of my success. I could have applied myself earlier in the semester and even enjoyed challenging myself through the work. I could have viewed the whole process as a character-building exercise instead of a burden.

When we practice more profound levels of self-awareness, we can observe our current ways of thinking, reflect on them, and open ourselves up to new positive thought patterns. We can start to slow down the reactive, emotional brain that constantly seeks comfort and approval, and introduce the smart brain, which is much more equipped for problem-solving.

Let me caveat this by saying that as a teenager, it's much more challenging to practice profound levels of self-awareness because you're still at a stage in life when so many variables are changing in and around you. It's natural for you to place more importance on other people's opinions and social media posts, so don't be hard on yourself when you do this exercise. The point is to notice why you do what you do so that if you *want* to change it, you can start taking those small steps in the right direction.

What's fun is when we become masters of self-awareness and start to recognize how much of what we think and do is just programmed into us! Most of our thoughts and actions are conditioned responses based on judgments we've formed that aren't necessarily true. If two people can have the same experience and feel two very different things about that same experience, it's possible your response to a situation is not the *only* response to that situation.

However, even just being able to reflect on why you're making the choices you're making, without doing anything differently, is a huge step in your progress toward empowerment.

For example, if I had a deeper level of self-awareness, I may have still bought those $250 pair of jeans in high school, but when they didn't give me the satisfaction I was looking for, maybe instead of moving on to the next trend, I would have realized that I was searching for acceptance in the wrong places and that the only place I was ever going to fulfill that need was within myself. I could have turned inward instead of continuing to look outward for temporary fixes.

Maybe if I had stopped to understand why I was dropping out of my math class, I would have tried a little harder before quitting. That way, even if I switched majors, I would have risen to the challenge sooner instead of wasting so much time ignoring the problem the second time around.

Asking yourself why you do the things you do on a daily basis is the number one most crucial component to improving your life. If we never questioned our poor decisions and reflected on what motivated us to make them, we would never actually learn from them! We'd simply shrug, walk away, stumble into a similar situation and undoubtedly repeat the same mistake. Take time in your daily life to ask why you are making the decisions you're making. You'll be fascinated by what you come up with.

WAS THERE A DIFFERENT CHOICE?

When you write down some of your recent decisions and the reasons behind those decisions, start exploring in your head if there was another choice you could have made if you had a different perspective about yourself or the world in that moment.

Maybe if you felt more confident in yourself, you would have raised your hand in class because other people's opinions of you wouldn't have had as much weight. Maybe instead of procrastinating for two hours on social media, you would have invested your time into something productive like learning a new skill or reading. And maybe when your friend asked you if she could copy your homework, you could have nicely explained why you didn't feel comfortable doing so.

Make sure you check in at the end of the week to go through some of your choices. Practice digging deeper into why you made those choices. Were they made because they felt like the best thing to do at the time? Or were they made because you were thinking about other people's perceptions of you (your friends, parents, classmates)? Perhaps they were choices you made because you didn't think you had any other options?

As you'll see later in this book, self-awareness is essential to unlocking all powerful change. It's hard to know where you're going if you don't know where you're starting from. When you develop self-awareness, you can identify the thoughts, beliefs, and behaviors you'd like to change so that you can work to shift them! The big question is: Do you have the courage to look at yourself honestly?

In the next chapter, you'll take the self-awareness to the next level as you start to observe your feelings.

3

OBSERVE YOUR FEELINGS

HOW TO CULTIVATE HEALTHY EMOTIONAL AWARENESS

> "To acquire knowledge, one must study; but to acquire wisdom, one must observe."
>
> — MARILYN VOS SAVANT

Now it's time to start applying self-awareness to your emotions. I won't lie. This is tough to do at any age. In fact, most people go their entire lives and never have the ability to observe their emotions honestly. However, being able to process our feelings in a healthy way is a critical component to our growth.

Emotional awareness is what we were practicing in the last chapter but stepped up a notch. You'll be asked to distance yourself from your emotional triggers *as* they are happening. So instead of rage posting about that horrible thing someone said to you on social media, you're going to take a step back, observe what you're feeling, and then ask questions about those feelings. In the age of texting, social media feeds, and triggers around every corner, observing your emotions can seem impossible, but that's why it's a game-changer.

Earlier in this book, we learned about the different centers of the brain—the logical, the emotional, and the survival brain. Emotional awareness will help us identify when we're becoming overwhelmed by the emotional brain and allow us to start activating the smart brain instead. Have you ever said or done something in the heat of the moment that you later regretted? This will help us avoid that.

In high school, I was in a very unhealthy relationship with a guy who wasn't the greatest (hey, we were kids). We were constantly fighting, breaking up, and getting back together. Fighting, breaking up and getting back together. On repeat.

On this particular day, when we broke up, I was sitting in my room talking to my friend on AOL instant messenger (our version of text messaging back in the day). She told me she overheard that my ex-boyfriend was going to take another girl out to see a movie that weekend. I immediately fell sick to my stomach. My heart started racing, and my head began to spin. Overcome with emotion, I made a beeline to the toilet and almost vomited. It felt like the whole world was crashing down on me.

I spent the next few weeks in total disorientation and grief over a situation I couldn't control. You might say that's a normal response for any teenager, and you're right. It might be "normal," but it certainly wasn't optimal. I had no tools to deal with my emotions in a healthy way.

When we're hit with intense emotions, sometimes we need go-to tools to stop ourselves from spinning out as quickly as possible. As I've personally discovered, physical exercises are the most practical and effective way to dissipate over-whelming emotion. They may feel unnatural to do at first, but if you take the time to do them, they become second nature. Soon, you'll be able to deal with intense emotions with more grace and maturity than you ever thought possible.

Here are some quick go-to exercises to help you get off the crazy train when you're feeling overwhelmed.

EXERCISES

DEEP BREATHING

You may have heard this suggestion at least a thousand times before, but that's because it works. Let me explain. When your emotional brain becomes activated due to stress, it sends signals to your survival brain to prepare you for the fight-flight-freeze response. Your heart rate beats faster, your palms sweat, and your breath quickens. Of course, you can't control your heart rate or sweat glands, but you *can* control your breathing.

This is why when you're in a state of emotional overwhelm, the most practical thing for you to do is to consciously regulate your breathing because it will send signals to the rest of your body to follow suit. Most people ignore this tip, but I recommend you try it now.

Take a deep breath into your chest and belly. Hold it in for five counts. Breathe out slowly, and hold it out for another five counts. Recycle and repeat as many times as possible until your body starts to calm and your heart rate slows.

This might feel unnatural when you're highly emotional, but taking active control of your breath is like a metaphor for taking active control of your life. Someone very smart once told me, "if you can't take control of your breath, it's pretty hard to take control of your life."

If you want to take this exercise to the next level, try the Wim Hof Method. I'll give you a basic explanation of this exercise here, but I recommend you do an online search of the "Wim Hof Method Breathing Exercise" to see live demonstrations.

Start by taking quick breaths into your nose while letting the exhale fall out of your mouth. Do this 30 times, focusing on your inhales. At the end of this cycle, breath out and hold your breath out for as long as possible. Next, breathe in and hold your breath in for ten seconds.

You should feel a tingling in your body when you're finished. That's called your life force, or "chi," as Chinese medicine calls it. From this place, you'll naturally find more distance from your emotional state.

TAPPING

Another exercise to play with is what's called "tapping." When you feel a strong emotional response coming on, or have anxious and negative thoughts, take your fingers and start to tap on different parts of your body while stating how you feel out loud. If you want to see this technique demonstrated, search for "EFT" or "The Tapping Solution" online.

This technique combines Chinese acupressure and modern psychology to help relieve emotional and psychological distress in your body by activating what's referred to as meridian points or energy channels. As strange as it sounds, this method is surprisingly effective at dissipating intense emotion and shifting the emotional state of your body.

Start by tapping on the outer edge of one hand, under your clavicle, right below your eyes, the corner of your eyes, the top of your head, your chin, your nose, and your armpit. As you tap, use enough force so you can feel your bone, but not too much force that it starts to hurt.

As you tap different parts of your body, speak your feelings out loud as intensely as they're coming up for you. Start with "Even though…" at the beginning of the exercise, and end with "I love and accept myself."

For instance, if I were to have applied this exercise to the situation with my ex-boyfriend, I would have started tapping on the edge of my hand and said: "Even though I'm pissed off that he's taking someone else out on a date," then I'd start tapping under my clavicle, "and it makes me feel sick," I'd move to the top of my head, "and I feel out of control in my body," tap under my eyes, "and mad at myself because I wish I didn't care so much," then move onto the top of my head again, "I love and accept myself."

When doing this, try recording how intense your emotions are on a scale of one to ten right before, and right after the exercise. You should notice a significant difference.

COLD SHOWERS

This may sound like something out of a bad teen movie, but it works. When we're anxious, we're so focused on the negative thoughts twirling around in our heads that we become totally disconnected from our bodies. Jumping into a cold shower instantly forces your mind away from it's spiraling and pulls you into the present moment. It acts like a "system interrupt."

Sometimes I find that even if it doesn't completely take away the sting of the emotions, it gives me enough distance to observe them for what they are so that I can better deal with them.

DROP YOUR HEAD

This is a simple exercise you can easily do whenever you feel overwhelmed. Sit in a chair, hang your head between your legs and breathe. Try it right now! Hang your head between your legs, close your eyes and count to twenty. As the blood rushes to your head, you'll feel your emotional brain start to slow down.

To be clear, these exercises are not designed to help you ignore your feelings or pretend like they don't exist. The last thing I want you to do is to pretend you aren't feeling what's coming up for you. In fact, numbing yourself to your emotions can be more detrimental in the long run, than letting them run wild.

The tools above are here to help you deal with the immediate sting of an intense emotional episode so that you can regain control over your mind and body again. From there, you are more able to confront your feelings honestly, rationally, and proactively.

Now that we've calmed down your emotional state, the following exercises will help you observe your emotions and see them for what they are and are not.

DOCUMENT THE EVENTS

The next time you find yourself in a situation with an intense emotional charge, pretend like you're documenting the events that just occurred, like an objective researcher. End the report with: "it made me feel [insert feeling], and my emotional brain kicked in."

Let me give you an example. You open your phone and scroll through social media. You see a story with your crush's arm around another girl—suddenly, your emotional brain kicks in. Your heart beats out of your chest, your face starts to burn, and you feel like you're about to scream. Instead of reaching for your phone and texting your friend in a panic, take a moment to report on the actual events that are happening.

It could go something like this:

I was at my desk trying to do homework when my mind started to wander, and I picked up my phone. I clicked on a story and saw a photo of my crush with his arm around another girl. It made me jealous and angry, and my emotional brain kicked in.

The last part of that statement, "It made me feel…and my emotional brain kicked in," is critical because it will help you cultivate the awareness of what's happening to you emotionally and what that emotion is doing to your physical body.

For instance, instead of stating "I'm angry," changing it to "It made me feel angry" will help you cultivate a deeper awareness that your emotional state is not who you are; it's just your reaction to the situation. Could those same given circumstances have made someone else feel relieved? It might be hard to believe, but yes. What if you later discovered that the person in the photo you saw was your crush's cousin? Would that have changed your emotional response? Yes.

Do you see how basing your sense of reality on emotions that could change at any moment isn't helpful? Just because you had an emotional reaction doesn't mean anything in your immediate circumstance has changed. Just as quickly as that emotional response came into you, it could disappear. You might say, "Well, something *has* changed because now I can't be with my crush!" I could say right back to you: "What if I told you that someone even better is going to show up tomorrow?"

When we end the statement with "and my emotional brain kicked in," we remind ourselves that it's not "us" making our hearts beat faster or turning our faces red. It's not *our* fault for feeling overwhelmed and anxious in the moment. The world may feel like it's ending in our bodies, but your smart brain knows that's not true and it will pass. When we realize that our emotional states are not always "smart," we can stop placing so much importance on them.

The quicker you can identify your emotions, the more distance you can have from them and accept them for what they are, and see them for what they're not. No matter how intense you may feel in the moment, you are not your grief. You are not your anxiety. You are not your fear. You are not your worry. You are not any current emotion that consumes you.

Now that you've taken the time to deal with your immediate emotional responses and have created some distance from them, it's time to ground yourself back into your physical body.

TUNE INTO YOUR SENSES

Wherever you find yourself, take mental inventory of what you can perceive with all five of your senses: sight, sound, taste, smell, and touch. Tuning into your physical surroundings will help you come back into the present moment.

If you were to speak this exercise out loud, it might sound like this:

I am in my room. I feel the chair under my legs. I smell cooking downstairs. I can see the carpet under my toes. I hear my mom's voice in the other room. I can taste my tongue.

By bringing your awareness back into your physical surroundings, you allow your emotional brain to differentiate what you are feeling vs. what is happening around you. This conscious separation between your thoughts, your emotions, and your physical reality is called mindfulness.

If I had practiced mindfulness in my earlier example involving my ex-boyfriend, I would have said something like:

I was sitting in my room messaging a friend on the computer. She said she overheard my ex-boyfriend taking someone else to the movies. It made me panic, and my emotional brain kicked in...But I am sitting in my chair. I can smell my hand cream. I can hear the murmuring of my sister downstairs. I see my computer screen in front of me. I can feel my shirt against my skin. I can taste my tongue.

I'll give another example of how this exercise could have helped me during an emotionally jarring situation. Freshman year, my two best friends decided to transfer to another school because it was closer to their parents. However, they waited until the end of the year to tell me because they were nervous about how I would react. When they finally told me, I let my emotional brain take over and blew up at them. Instead of having an honest conversation about what was happening, I cut them out of my life cold turkey.

Not once did I take a second to pause, gather my thoughts and feelings and consider the situation objectively. Not once did I let myself process the vulnerability and hurt of what was happening. Instead, I did the two things that I regret to this day. Firstly, I let my emotional brain take over and reacted to the situation in an irrational way. And secondly, I bottled up all those feelings of sadness and hurt I was going through and pretended like they didn't exist.

If I had taken a moment to calm my emotional brain and objectively think about the whole situation, I would have realized that they weren't trying to hurt me. In fact, it made logical sense for them to move to another school. Additionally, there was nothing I could have done to change the situation. The only thing I had control over was how I chose to respond to it.

I never did see them again. Suffice to say, that following summer was a very lonely one.

But like that math class example I gave earlier, you can't escape life lessons; you can only defer them to a later date. Years later, when I was finally unpacking my childhood trauma, I found myself balling my eyes out about losing two best friends I never spoke to again. I had buried away those emotions and memories so deeply that I was only able to come to terms with them years later.

Being able to process your emotions proactively allows you to distance yourself from the immediate overwhelm of a situation and move forward with emotional maturity and strength. It also prevents you from reacting in ways that are unhealthy, and you might later regret. The added benefit is that you won't have to wait years before being able to heal from that situation.

Here are some tell-tale signs that you might want to practice these exercises:

- Something that someone says or does "triggers" you into an emotion.
- You feel emotionally overwhelmed by a situation and can't think clearly.
- You start to blame someone for how you feel.
- Even worse, you begin to take it out on them.

Developing emotional self-awareness builds maturity and strength. You can communicate more effectively with others because you're less reactive and defensive. People will be more forthright and honest with you because they know you can handle it. You can also demonstrate more compassion for other people since you're less preoccupied with your own emotions. As you practice self-awareness and distance yourself from your reactive mind, you start to emanate an internal resilience that people naturally gravitate towards.

THE IMPORTANCE OF DISCIPLINE

Now you might be thinking, how can these exercises be done under so much intense emotion? There's no way I will remember these steps when I'm anxious, angry, or stressed out!

Put these exercises somewhere you can refer back to quickly. Write them down on a piece of paper and tape them to your mirror or above your dresser. Nothing is stopping you from changing your life, besides you!

Too often, friends and family members come to me for advice, and when I give it to them, they thank me but rarely take it. They say something like, "But that's just not me" or "I don't have the time for that." And guess what? A few weeks later, they'll come back looking for advice about the same situation! They never change, their lives never change, and their problems worsen.

It's your life and entirely your choice, but if you're reading this book, you wanted to get something out of it. You wanted to improve some part of your experience or learn how to be a healthier, more resilient version of yourself. But guess what? Ultimately, you and only you have the power to do that. I can give you tools and advice, but you have to have the discipline to apply them.

I used to hate self-improvement books. I was either too full of myself or too lazy (or both) to take their advice and do the exercises they suggested. Even though I knew something inside of me needed to change, I couldn't apply the discipline to do anything differently than what I was already doing. It took me a whole decade to realize the truth behind Einstein's insanity quote—that doing the same thing over and over again would only lead me to the same results! So here I am, over a decade later, telling you to do what I didn't have the foresight to do at your age.

So if you skimmed through those previous exercises, I highly encourage you to go back and write them down. Put them somewhere you can easily find them! At the very least, bookmark those pages so that when you decide that you want to do things differently, you can.

Like I said in the beginning, I'm not promising you an easy solution for anxiety, stress, or challenges in your life. What I can give you is the ability to shift your perspective so you can deal with them in an empowered state. If you meet me halfway and have the discipline to apply the concepts in this book, your life experience *will* start to change. You *will* become a more empowered person.

Now that I've sufficiently lectured you about discipline, let's dive deeper into observing your thoughts and emotions and how they can help us build empowerment.

4

FEELINGS AS TOOLS

HOW FEELINGS CAN HELP YOU BECOME EMPOWERED

"Your feelings are your greatest tools to help you create your life."

— RHONDA BYRNE

In the last chapter, we learned how to become aware of our feelings, deal with them in the moment, and gain objectivity from them. While they don't define who we are, they deserve respect for the information they can provide us. Emotions can be a great tool to help us identify aspects of ourselves that need a little work.

As a teenager, letting people see you "too" excited, sad, or emotional is not cool. Many times people push down their feelings and pretend they "don't care" about anything (not even about themselves). Unfortunately, numbing yourself to your emotions doesn't heal the triggers that created them in the first place. It just buries them deeper inside of you.

I know someone who conditioned herself never to show her emotions when she was a teen, and 10+ years later, she now struggles with honestly expressing herself in her relationships. Whenever she gets emotionally overwhelmed, she either covers it up with anger or runs away. She never stops to consider that her emotions might be telling her something. I suggest you start listening to your emotions—even the "bad" ones.

Have you heard the expression: "What we resist, persists?" It's true. What we ignore dealing with today only comes to bite us in the butt tomorrow. And the lesson is usually more brutal the longer we wait to learn it.

Having emotional integrity and honesty is a trait that will serve you in every relationship you'll ever have–with your family, romantic partner, friends, and colleagues. I can't tell you how often I've seen relationships fall apart because someone didn't know how to be emotionally honest. I've seen business partnerships crumble because neither party could get over their pride and express themselves candidly.

So let me repeat myself: feelings are not wrong! When we allow them to control our lives they become problematic. However, when used properly, emotions can act as tools for growth. The "good" feelings can tell us that we're on the right path (doesn't apply to temporary fixes), and the "negative" emotions can give us indications of what we need to address.

When I was younger, I was always frustrated about my weight. My feelings about my body ranged from angry to sad, and the thoughts accompanying them were some variation of "you're not good enough." I was an average size for my age, but no matter how many times other people would tell me that there was nothing wrong with me, I didn't believe them.

My biggest mistake was that I didn't understand the message my negative emotions were trying to tell me. I thought my negative emotions were telling me that I needed to "fix" myself and get skinnier. So I started going on unhealthy diets. I skipped my mom's homemade lunches. I took diet pills. However, when I *did* lose the weight, those negative feelings just grew inside of me. My mood suffered, my energy dropped, and it became harder to focus in class. I became even more obsessed with my weight!

If I had practiced emotional awareness and dissected the root cause of my frustration, I would have realized that it wasn't my weight that was the problem; it was my thinking that I had a weight problem that was the problem! My negative feelings about my body were not trying to get me to lose weight; they were trying to get me to address my low self-worth. Deep down, I held onto an internalized belief that I wasn't "good enough" compared to my peers.

If I had taken the time to analyze and observe my feelings objectively and rationally, I would have spent more time addressing my low self-esteem and less time abusing myself with negative thoughts about my body. If I *did* want to lose weight, I wouldn't have approached it from a place of self-hatred and abuse but a state of self-love and patience.

Let's revisit the example of my ex-boyfriend taking another girl out to the movies. As I said, I didn't handle the situation very well. I let my emotional brain take over, which completely spun me out of control, and for the next few weeks, I was living in a constant state of heightened anxiety.

If I had used the tools we talked about in the last chapter, I would have:

1. Dealt with the emotional overwhelm through exercises like deep breathing.
2. Documented the events that led to the trigger as objectively as possible.
3. Stated how the events made me feel and added, "and my emotional brain took over."
4. Connected with my five senses to bring myself back into my physical body.

These exercises wouldn't have totally dissipated the jealousy and hurt I felt. Still, they would have grounded me back to a place of more reason and rationality to move forward.

Let's take this example one step further.

EXERCISES

JOURNAL YOUR FEELINGS

This isn't the kind of journaling they teach in kindergarten. This is a "getting all those nasty thoughts and feelings" out on paper, sort of journaling. It's almost the journaling equivalent of finger painting. In fact, when you're done with the exercise, there's no need to keep what you wrote. You can shred the paper and throw it away.

This journaling exercise is about respecting your feelings for what they are and what they are not and using them to gain perspective. In other words, it's about using the self-awareness you've been developing in the earlier chapters to help propel you forward. After practicing this exercise every day for years, journaling is, hands down, one of the most life-changing activities I continue to do daily.

So here's the exercise: Get out a notebook and write down your thoughts and feelings in the most honest, vulnerable, and raw way possible. It doesn't have to sound pretty, contain whole sentences, or make sense. It can be messy, weird, grammatically incorrect, and nonsensical. The point is to face your uncomfortable feelings and thoughts by getting them out in front of you. Don't think too hard.

Once you're done, you might notice that you brain-dumped about a few situations in your life, but there is likely one that stands out more than the rest. Looking at that one situation or issue, answer the following question: "What's the deeper reason I feel this way?" From there, you'll ask yourself a few more questions as outlined below.

To demonstrate, let's apply this exercise to my previous example.

My Initial brain dump could have looked like this:

I feel so upset. How could he do this to me? What a horrible person. I hate him! I wish I had never met him. How could he move on so fast? He probably thinks she's prettier than me. Am I that forgettable? The thought of seeing them at school makes me feel so sick. Gross!! I'm so pissed.

After further consideration, I'd ask myself: **"What's the deeper reason I feel this way?"**

I feel this way because his seeing another girl makes me feel insignificant, unwanted, lonely, and small. The fact that he was able to move on so fast makes me feel like I didn't mean anything to him. What did I do wrong? That girl must be better than me in every way. I'm scared that I'm not good enough.

Then, go even deeper: **"And because of this, what's the worst thing that could happen?"**

No one will ever love me again. I will have lost the love of my life. I will be totally embarrassed at school.

Then, go a little further, and ask, **"Is any of that true?"**

Probably not. I'm only 16, so I'll probably fall in love again. He probably isn't the love of my life since we had so many fights and kept breaking up. I might feel embarrassed and hurt at school if I see them together, though.

Then ask yourself: **"Is this still going to matter in five years? Ten years?"**

No, it won't matter in 5 or 10 years. I'll be out of high school and even out of college. Who knows what my life is going to look like in five or ten years.

Finally, reflect: **"Can I change my mindset going forward from this experience?"**

I can look at the bigger picture of the situation. The fact is, we broke up for a reason because we were constantly fighting, and he didn't treat me the way I wanted to be treated. This was my first relationship, and to be honest, it probably won't be my last. Over the next few years, I'll be onto another stage of my life, and I probably won't even think about this anymore. It still hurts a lot right now, but I know these feelings will pass.

Taking the time to follow these prompts and observe your situation objectively is not easy, but that's why it can be so life-changing.

Let's take another example from my high school days.

I managed to get on the varsity tennis team during my freshman year of high school because my dad loved the sport and spent summers practicing with me. I don't know how much I liked the sport myself, but I knew I didn't want to disappoint my dad, and I "needed" a sport to put on my college applications. However, I faced a two-fold issue: I was a poor loser and wasn't good under pressure. So, what did I do to "escape" feelings of failure? I self-sabotaged.

I'd get myself into a foul mood before the game, throw a fit, make an excuse, and lose as quickly as possible by either swinging my racket as hard as I could or not running after the ball at all. In my mind, I would rather fail on *my* terms than put in actual effort and still lose. After the game, I'd go home and do my best to numb the pain of defeat.

Suppose I had more self-awareness of my thoughts and feelings at the time. In that case, I could have addressed them head-on and actively searched for what they were trying to tell me instead of numbing myself and avoiding them. I could have turned those four years on the tennis team from a frustrating self-defeating experience into a fun and positive one.

Unfortunately, I ended up doing the opposite. Instead of examining my feelings and digging deep into what was going on with me, I chose to ignore the emotional turmoil that was brewing under the surface in the hopes that one day it would all be over. Of course, high school did end, and so did my time on the tennis team, but unfortunately, the habit of self-sabotage lingered well into my twenties. Whenever I couldn't handle the emotional pressure of certain situations in my life, I'd either give up prematurely or shoot myself in the foot so I wouldn't have to face the disappointment.

If I were doing this exercise using my tennis team experience from high school, it might have looked something like this.

Write down your thoughts and feelings.

Ugh, I'm so angry that I lost AGAIN. I hate tennis. It's such a stupid sport. Why did my dad want me to play it? I'm so annoyed at him. I can't wait until it's over.

What's the deeper reason you feel this way?

The deeper reason why I feel so pissed off about losing is that it makes me look bad. I feel embarrassed that I lost in front of my teammates and in front of my dad. I feel ashamed of myself and feel like a loser.

And because of this, what's the worst thing that could happen?

If people see me as a loser, they won't like me. And if they don't like me, I'll be alone. If I'm alone, I'll have no friends. And if my dad is disappointed, he won't be proud of me. If he's not proud of me, he won't think I have as much value, and he won't love me as much.

Is any of that true?

People on my tennis team might be bummed and not like me anymore. My dad has always been there for me and loved me, even before I played tennis, so he will still love me as much as he does now. My value is not defined by whether I win or lose a tennis match.

Is this still going to matter in 5 years? Ten years?

Probably not because I would have forgotten about this game by then, and I'm going to be out of high school, anyway.

Can I change my mindset going forward from this experience?

The only thing I can do is try my best, and if people on my tennis team don't like me because I lose a game, they're not my friends.

Maybe the reason I'm not trying my best in my matches is because I'm scared of looking stupid and failing. But if I don't try, I will fail, anyway. Maybe I should try harder and go for it instead of giving up so easily. I know that giving up on myself before even trying isn't a good habit.

Can you see how writing your thoughts and feelings down using pen and paper can be helpful? When we bottle up our emotions, they get trapped in an emotional loop in our bodies because they have nowhere else to go! When we identify with these loops for too long, we accept them as truth, and we tend to create the same kinds of experiences over and over again in our lives.

When we brain dump our thoughts and feelings onto a piece of paper, we can read them, study them, analyze them, and poke holes in them. This makes it easier for us to see them for what they are—thoughts and feelings that we're currently experiencing but do not define us. It allows us to see how misleading and harmful they can be if we let them continue without interruption. The exciting part of being able to distance ourselves from our negative mental loops is that we can start to choose something different.

Trying my best in a tennis match and losing would have felt bad in the moment, but at least I wouldn't have had any regrets. Learning how to give something my best effort, no matter how embarrassed I was of failing, would have been a powerful life lesson that I wish I had dared to learn at the time.

Let's take my earlier example when it came to my negative body image.

Write down all of your thoughts and feelings.

I hate my body. It doesn't look thin enough, and I want to be thinner so I can be more attractive and feel better in front of my friends.

What's the deeper reason you feel this way?

Because I don't look like the popular girls at my school, and people don't see me as pretty, making me feel invisible. If I had a thinner body, I'd be able to prove to my classmates that I am hot. Boys will like me, and I won't be overlooked or disrespected.

And because of this, what's the worst thing that could happen?

If I'm not prettier, boys won't like me, I will continue to feel bad about myself, and girls will continue to be mean to me. I'll never know what it's like to be good enough!

Is any of that true?

Probably not. I'll probably find a partner at some point in my life. I also don't know if people would treat me any differently if I changed the way I looked, and even if they did, I don't know if the relationships would be meaningful.

Is this still going to matter in five years? Ten years?

I probably won't be around the same people in a few years, so that everything could change.

Can I change my mindset in the future from this experience?

Maybe I think that changing my body will improve my life and people will like me more, but I don't even know if that's true. I could have a different appearance but still be treated exactly the same. So maybe I'm putting too much importance on something that doesn't matter as much as I think.
Obsessing about my appearance just makes me feel bad about myself. Why can't I feel worthy with how I look now? Plenty of people who don't look like supermodels are successful and have confidence. Maybe confidence and feeling worthy are about more than just appearance. Maybe I should stop obsessing so much about my weight and focus on other things.

Writing your thoughts down and distancing yourself from a situation that feels intense takes a lot of maturity, patience, and time. Too often, we want to ignore our emotions in favor of easy distractions–texts, social media, TV. But the sooner we take time to confront our thoughts and feelings in a productive, positive way, the much better off our lives will be.

After regularly doing this exercise, you will see how much you are NOT your thoughts or feelings (yes, no matter how strong they are). You'll be able to face and even embrace your feelings and know they're just opportunities to become a better, wiser, stronger, and more resilient version of you.

Getting honest about the thoughts and feelings I was holding inside was challenging, especially in the beginning. I'd write something down and cringe, thinking, *"Wow, do I really want to admit that?"* But after a while, I prided myself on being as honest, authentic, and vulnerable as possible with myself. The mentality became: "The more honest, vulnerable, and raw I am on the page right now, the more brave, strong, and whole I will become."

A teacher once told me that the goal in life isn't to avoid discomfort; it's to get more comfortable with being uncomfortable. That couldn't be more true. You will never escape feelings of discomfort. That's simply a necessary part of life. From here on out, I encourage you to stop seeking comfort and embrace growth from the uncomfortable.

In the next chapter, we'll help all of you overthinkers out there quiet the monkey mind and stop it before it takes over.

5

TAME THE STORY MONSTER

HOW TO STOP THE NEGATIVE NARRATIVES
THAT HOLD YOU BACK

> "Stop the mental chatter about what's wrong and what's not complete. There is a presence of Love that is seeking to express itself through you."
>
> — MICHAEL BECKWITH

Have you ever been embarrassed and shortly after felt a rush of blood to your face? Have you ever gotten mad at the thought of a situation and felt your chest heat up seconds later? Negative thoughts tend to snowball, leading to more thoughts, and then more thoughts, until we have walked so far down a path of negative thinking that we totally lose control over our state of being.

In the last few chapters, we discussed how to immediately deal with intense emotional responses and then reflect on how to best handle that particular life situation in a more productive way. What about those little neurotic thoughts we have throughout the day? You know, those nagging stories we tell ourselves about other people and the world around us that bully us into feeling small?

When you're feeling triggered by something that comes up–a passing comment by a friend, an unpleasant exchange with a teacher, or bad news on a test, it only takes 90 seconds for it to pass through your body, according to Dr. Jill Bolte Taylor. That's 90 seconds for an emotion to switch on, move through your body, and flush away. What does that tell us? That you are actually perpetuating any negative emotion that lingers in you for longer than 90 seconds!

This leads us to the good news: we have control over whether we let those negative reactions flush out of our system in those 90 seconds or whether we invite them to stay longer. Unfortunately, most of us are hardwired to let them last longer than they need to.

In high school, I was a classic overthinker. I would read into every situation and make up elaborate stories in my head about "what it all meant." If the tone of a teacher sounded a little impatient, my mind would scroll through a list of all the reasons I could have offended her. If a friend decided to sit with another group of peers at lunch, my brain would go into a monologue: *I can't believe she's sitting there today. Why didn't she invite me? Does she think I'm not cool enough to sit with them? Maybe she's embarrassed by me. Maybe she doesn't like me, and she doesn't think I'm cool anymore. I bet she's talking about me behind my back. I shouldn't have told her all of those secrets last week! Oh, no, she's going to tell the whole school! I can't believe she'd do that!*

We all feed the story monster. Whether that's about your clothes, how you walk, talk, what you text, or how someone looks at you in the halls. We get triggered by one tiny event, circumstance, or interaction, and our emotional brains switch on and give us supporting evidence as to why we should feed that situation more energy than it deserves. The problem is if we don't catch the emotional brain before it goes haywire, we believe its stories, and those stories start to dictate our lives. That rarely leads to a good outcome.

However, suppose we know that we have a whole 90 seconds to cut the story monster off from getting carried away. That means we have the opportunity to redirect our thoughts into a more rational state and prevent our emotional minds from running the show. Sounds easy, but as you can imagine, it's much harder in practice.

As I came to find out, the most challenging part of this process was making the conscious decision to *want* to stop the story monster. I knew I had the power to prevent it from ruining my day, but part of me *wanted* it to keep running. Feeding the story monster can feel addicting and almost satisfying because making up stories in our heads gives us the false impression that we're somehow taking control over the situation and "figuring out" a solution to the problem. Yes, even a problem that might not exist.

How often have you spent hours in your head dissecting a text message or a five-second interaction trying to find some resolution or understanding about what it all meant? Was it necessary? Helpful? Productive? Or did it introduce further anxiety, emotional stress and use unnecessary energy? And how many times have you invented a narrative in your head around a situation, only to find out that none of your assumptions were actually true? Exactly.

When I started my Youtube channel, most of the comments on my videos were from a very small, supportive group. One day, I remember an unusual comment on a video that said something like, "Must be really hot to wear that," about a tank top I was wearing. At the time, I was conditioned to receive positive comments, so I just assumed it was positive. I remember replying, "Yes, it gets hot over here in LA!"

It wouldn't be until a year later that I met that person in real life, and she would admit that she was trying to poke fun at my fashion choices! She told me that my positive reply to her snarky comment changed her opinion of me, and that's why she decided to follow and support my content. She even told me I became one of her inspirations for creating her own content!

Now, if I had assumed that she was being snarky (which was confirmed in this case), I would have triggered the story monster and replied something very snarky back. But because I didn't have the time to let myself ruminate over the various negative narratives in my head, I just assumed the best, which completely changed the situation's outcome in real life.

Assuming the worst in social situations to protect yourself from future harm only ends up robbing yourself of the present moment, taking away your joy, and shrinking your experience of the world around you. And on top of that, it rarely keeps you safe.

Have there been times in your life when you let the story monster take hold and let you believe the worst about a person or a situation? Did it ever lead to a positive outcome? We have more control over our narratives than we think. So, instead of becoming a victim of the worst-case scenarios, why don't we become the creators of the best ones?

This doesn't mean living in a fairyland and not using your sense of judgment in situations that are openly abusive or physically dangerous. Still, it *does* mean taking a second to observe your reactions and asking yourself if your conclusions are accurate, justified, and, most importantly, helpful.

I'll give you another example. In college, I was working on a creative project where I assumed this one person had something against me. Anytime I'd speak, I felt like he would cut me off. I didn't feel like he was treating me with as much respect as the other collaborators in the group. It not only made me frustrated, but it ticked me off. My story monster fired up, and I started angrily spinning out about this person. I began venting to people around me: "Who does this awful, sexist guy think he is?"

While I was in the middle of a rant, my friend asked, "What if he *is* sexist and doesn't like you? Does focusing on his sexism and the fact that he might not like you help the situation?" I considered, "No." "Does focusing on it make him any less sexist?" "No." "Does focusing on it make you any better of a collaborator?" "No." "Then why are you focusing so much energy on it?" I didn't have an answer to that other than, "Because it makes me angry!"

I hated to admit it, but he was right. It did me no good to stay focused on the story that I was creating in my head. I had to let it go–not just for our project but for my own peace of mind.

He then added: "Why don't you focus on the positive outcome of the project? How does that feel?" "Better." "Instead of wasting your energy and time on something you *don't* want, why not focus all that energy on the things you *do* want?"

The kicker of the whole situation was that I still, to this day, have no idea if that guy had anything against me or if he *was* sexist. In the end, it didn't matter. The only thing that the story monster gave me was a few days of raised blood pressure, increased stress, and wasted energy.

Permitting yourself to let go of negative narratives and redirect that energy into something positive is one of the biggest keys to living an empowered life. You'll be less willing to give anyone else the power to ruin your day, make you feel small, or discourage you, because you won't allow them. You'll begin to take active control over who and what you let affect you.

It takes conscious and deliberate effort to catch a spiraling narrative, hit pause, and stop it in its tracks. Throw in anxiety, stress, and nerves, and it becomes even more challenging. But learning how to tame the story monster and, even better, redirect that focus into something you *do* want is one of the most profound life skills you can master.

Below are some simple but effective exercises to help you catch the story monster when it rears its ugly head and put an end to it.

EXERCISE

"Get Out"

This exercise is almost too easy to be effective, but it works. The next time you find yourself spinning out about something in your head, stop whatever you're doing. Give a command to your thoughts and say: "Get out." Then imagine a squeegee physically wiping your mind clean.

If the unhelpful thoughts reappear, repeat this exercise. You may find that you have to do this ten or even 20 times before the thoughts subside, but the more you practice it, the more effective it is. Like training a puppy, she might need to hear a command multiple times, but at some point, she will listen.

When you're by yourself, you can even use your hands to push the thoughts out of your space while shouting, "Get out!!" You might feel crazy doing it, but boy, does it work! I suggest you try it out for fun. When you give yourself permission to really let yourself go with this exercise, you'll have the added benefit of releasing stagnant energy in your body that you didn't even know you were holding onto.

By the way, you can still use this technique when you're in a room full of people. Instead of saying "get out" out loud, just say it in your head and imagine the squeegee wiping your mind blank. I love this exercise because it's so simple and gets easier to use the more you use it!

Journal it out

Another exercise you can do when your monkey mind starts to take over is to journal it out. Start by writing down your train of thoughts on a piece of paper. Let it all out and let it be as messy as possible. Keep writing until you feel like there's nothing more to say.

Then ask yourself the following questions:

1. Do I know for a fact that all of this is 100% true?
2. Is this train of thought or story helpful for me and the situation?
3. Is it making me more productive, healthier, or happier to indulge these thoughts?

You will inevitably conclude that most of your stories are just stories. Moreover, indulging in those stories is rarely helpful for any given situation, whether or not they are true! So, if a train of thought isn't helpful, isn't 100% true, and doesn't make you happier, what good does it do to hold onto them? It's like wasted storage space on your phone.

When you finally practice how to stop the story monster, your mind becomes easier and easier to train. At first, it will feel like an uphill battle, and you *will* have a lot of internal resistance, but like any skill, the goal is to commit yourself to the process so that it eventually becomes a habit.

6

MEAN PEOPLE

AN IMPORTANT MESSAGE FOR THOSE WHO ARE BULLIED

This is a short chapter dedicated to those who experience bullying

Once in a while you may run into people who deliberately try to hurt you or make you feel small. As a teen, it's something that happens more frequently than parents realize. I know, because it happened to me throughout my childhood and high school years.

When I was younger I was obsessed with the movie *The Lion King*. I was SO obsessed with the film that I even bought the sing-a-long book and learned the lyrics to every song by heart. I remember belting "I Just Can't Wait to Be King" in the backseat of the car, while forcing my parents to turn off the radio. That birthday, when my grandmother gifted me a sweatshirt with Simba on it, I was so excited to wear it to school.

The next day at recess, two girls pushed me on the ground and shouted: "Ew, what a stupid sweatshirt!" In an attempt to avoid them, I hid in the girl's bathroom and locked myself in a stall. A few seconds later, I heard them follow me in. They started to kick the stall door and scream obscenities. I don't remember what they said exactly, but I vividly remember the fear and confusion I felt as I cowered silently with my eyes closed. "What did I do wrong?" I asked myself.

Whether it was because my ears were too big, or my eyes were "too small," or my clothes were weird, I often found myself getting singled out in class. In high school, it wasn't that much different. People played pranks on me and called me names. It felt like everyday was a battlefield.

Without realizing it, I ended up internalizing a lot of these negative encounters and I did the worst thing you can do when bullying happens. I blamed *myself* thinking that I was doing something wrong or that somehow *I* was wrong.

In reality, there was nothing wrong with me. And if you experience similar bullying, there is nothing wrong with you. Mean people are mean because they are so hurt and sad on the inside that they can only feel good about themselves by making other people feel small. I know that might be hard to understand, but if you've ever been mean to someone, you know this is the truth.

Here's my biggest message to you: Do NOT let these sad people give you reason to abuse yourself. Do NOT let their words about you, become yours. Do NOT let them keep you small, or convince you that you are any less worthy in life. It's a big lie. And if you let that lie take ahold of you, you will deprive yourself of the beauty that you are, and end up a victim to their cruelty.

Only recently have I begun to understand how deeply I took on those encounters and allowed them to diminish me throughout my life. I don't want the same for you. Rise above them, and use them as fuel to become the most empowered, unapologetic version of yourself possible. The tools in this book will help you get there.

In the next chapter, we'll learn how to retrain your brain to think more positively about yourself and the world around you which can lead to amazing transformation.

7

RETRAIN YOUR BRAIN

REWIRE YOUR BRAIN FOR SUCCESS AND HAPPINESS

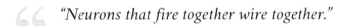 *"Neurons that fire together wire together."*

— *DEEPAK CHOPRA*

L et's explore how we can reprogram that chatterbox to something more positive, shall we? We have a brain for a reason. Without it, we wouldn't be able to take exams, write papers, text our friends, and post cute photos on social media. But as we've explored, it often goes off the rails and starts a life of its own (not a very fun one).

According to the National Science Foundation, an average person has about 12,000 to 60,000 thoughts per day, and they estimate that approximately 80% of those are negative. It's no wonder we're so easily stressed and anxious. I mean, what a painful existence!

Neuroscience has been asking over the years whether it's possible to reprogram our brains. Can we change the wiring of our thoughts from being negatively skewed to positively skewed? The research has been promising, and we'll leverage it in this chapter.

There was a girl in my high school who glowed with positivity everywhere she went. She greeted the world with a radiant smile, and the world smiled right back. It wasn't surprising that she was one of the most popular kids in our class, but she was different than the other popular girls. She didn't have to be mean or cruel to get the respect of her peers. Everyone just felt good in her presence.

Meanwhile, there I was, constantly second-guessing myself. Instead of radiating positivity and rainbows, I shrank in my seat, hoping to survive fifth period. I remember sitting in class looking at that girl and thinking, "How is it possible for someone to be so confident in her skin?"

To this day, I still don't know whether her cheery disposition was just an act, but it did beg the question in my mind: "How can I interact with the world like that? What's stopping ME from being that radiant?"

After high school, I'd come across people like that girl from my class every so often. People who could light up a room because they were lit up on the inside. People who didn't have to try to fit in because they weren't in their heads wondering *how* to fit in. People who could interact with anyone with ease because they saw the world around them as a positive place to explore, not a traumatic place they wanted to avoid.

More interestingly, I also noticed something else about these people. They were the people who seemed to attract a lot of "luck" in their lives–whether in careers, relationships, friendships, or cool experiences. They weren't the most talented, attractive or intelligent people. They were just a natural magnet for good things.

Coincidence? Possibly. Or did their positive perception of themselves somehow affect their lived reality? Take me, for instance. I worked hard, was bright, and applied myself–so why weren't all these good things happening for me in the way they were happening for them?

When we were babies, we cried after pooping our pants, became frustrated when we were hungry, and got angry when toys were taken away from us. Still, we were utterly uninhibited in expressing joy, exuberance, and laughter. We had an effervescent quality that made people *want* to be around us, hold us, and take care of us. This quality is what I like to call the glow of limitless possibilities.

It's important to remember that this isn't some foreign concept to who you are right now. You *were* that joy, spark, and effervescence at one point. In fact, it's your most natural state of being. Over the years, however, that light started to dim when we were introduced to stress, peer pressure, and social anxiety. We forgot about the bright souls we were, and our brains started to rewire toward self-doubt, low self-worth, negativity, and pessimism.

As mentioned at the beginning of this chapter, research shows that our brains have neuroplasticity, or the ability to rewire themselves. Attitudes and outlooks in life are more malleable than we once thought, and there are ways we can condition our brains to become more "naturally" optimistic and positive. So, instead of assuming we won't be able to pass that next math exam, we'll start thinking, "If I put in the effort, I can definitely pass that test!"

Let me caveat my following points by stating that in no way is the goal in life to be a big smiling ball of sunshine 24/7. That's simply impossible, inauthentic, and boring. We are human beings which means we are gifted with the capacity to express the whole spectrum of emotions. Without sadness, would we even know what happiness feels like?

What I *am* posing is the possibility of retraining our brains from being 80% negative to, let's say, 60% positive. Imagine going through your day feeling optimistic and excited about the future ahead of you instead of feeling stuck and anxious about surviving the week. Now *that* is a goal worth shooting for.

When I was younger, I had a bad habit of assuming the worst outcome of any social situation. The homecoming dance was right around the corner, and I dreaded it. Not only was I going alone, but I became mentally conditioned to view school dances as another opportunity to feel awkward. Instead of approaching the dance as a fun experience to enjoy with my friends, I approached it like an obligation I needed to "get over with."

When I entered the auditorium, I could feel my body shrink. "Here we go," I thought. My friends, on the other hand, were determined to have a good time. They ran to the dance floor and encouraged me to join them, but I'd shake my head and pretend to be finishing my can of Coke. The outcome of the night? My friends laughed, danced, and enjoyed themselves, and I was left feeling sorry for myself.

I probably don't need to tell you what went wrong here, but that whole situation could have played out very differently if I had approached it with a mindset that wasn't wired toward self-doubt, pessimism, and a bad outcome.

I'd like to think there's an alternative reality where I said, "I'm nervous about going to this dance, but what if I have a really good time with my friends? What if we laugh, giggle, and make the most of this cool experience? I'm excited to find out!" I still might have gone to the dance nervous, but in *this* reality, there would have been excitement in my belly as I approached the auditorium. I would have been open to experiencing the best outcome of the night. Maybe, I would have danced, laughed, and remembered that night as a special memory with old friends. I will never know.

Negative thinking and assuming the worst is something that many people suffer from, so if you experience this, you're not alone. However, that doesn't mean it can't or shouldn't be changed. The problem with pessimistic thinking is that it prepares your body to act according to what it expects. If you expect to do poorly on an upcoming test, guess what? You're less likely to study hard because you're already preparing for a bad outcome. When you get the test back with a disappointing grade, you'll throw your arms up and say: "See? I knew I wasn't good at taking tests!"

Likewise, if you expect a social situation will be awkward? You're probably going to make it *more* awkward because you're expecting that outcome. Therefore, any perceived awkwardness in the situation will magnify. It won't be long before you walk away from the interaction, thinking: "I knew it! I'm always so awkward!" Thus, reinforcing the negative feedback loop once again.

When I was introduced to this concept of rewiring my brain, my first objection was: "Is this even going to work? I mean, I'm not a neuroscientist." After I started the process and saw some results, my subsequent objections became, "Well, even if I become more optimistic and let go of my negative self-talk, will anything actually change in my life?" I resisted this idea for years until I fully committed myself, and my life *did* start to change.

Let me give you an example. Let's say you want to be friends with someone but feel too shy to go up to them and introduce yourself. What if you heard through rumors that this person wanted to be friends with you, too? Wouldn't you think: "Well, this is definitely going to go well!" You'd probably be much more willing to go up to that person and make a new friend.

On the flip side, let's say you heard from your peers that the person you wanted to meet didn't like meeting new people and was rumored to be kind of mean. You might think: "Hmm, maybe I should play it safe and save myself the rejection."

Now imagine the rumors your peers told you were thoughts in your head. Can you see the trickle effect this might have on your life?

I want to make it clear, however, that positive thinking is not supposed to be the key to getting your way all the time. Nothing in life is supposed to go your way 100% of the time, and nothing ever should! We'd never grow or learn or develop. What I will say, however, is that when you think more positively about yourself and the future ahead, success feels more promising. Rejection seems less daunting. And trying your best is not a waste; it's a strengthening opportunity. You also increase your odds of attracting the right people, situations, and experiences that will benefit you.

When I began switching my internal script from pessimism and defeatism to optimism and excitement, the physical nature of my reality began changing. Opportunities started showing up, people were more interested in being around me, and my overall experience was much more fun. Anything "negative" that showed up was that much easier to navigate.

The real gift of rewiring your brain to think more positively is improving your general life experience. You become "naturally" wired to see the good, the progress, and the possibility of life, instead of getting caught up in the doubts, the negative, and the challenges.

Believe it or not, some people actually *want* to keep their negative thinking because they think it protects them from disappointment (for example, me, ten years ago). The thought is: "Well, if I always expect the worst, at least I can never be disappointed."

Unfortunately, as I discovered for many years, this never saves you from the pain of disappointment. Your brain ends up using every disappointing event as evidence as to why your life will suck and never change.

I will also caution you that the longer we let our brains go down the path of negative thinking, the harder it is to steer the car around. You see, when our minds and bodies react to stimuli in a certain way over and over again, we create what are called neural pathways in the brain, or what I like to call "roads of least resistance," whereby the brain gets so used to going down that same negative path, it becomes a natural reaction. Suppose this happens over a long enough period– months, years, maybe even decades. In that case, those neural pathways become so ingrained that we eventually think all those negative assumptions are true and not what we've been programmed to see.

From middle school up until my late twenties, I trained myself to expect the worst in situations, especially about outcomes I cared about. I'd beat myself up when I was delivered bad news and say, "See, I knew it. I knew I wasn't good enough." It became strangely comforting to expect the worst because at least I could never disappoint myself. It helped justify to my friends, family, and most of all, to myself why I should stay small and never dream big. In the much larger picture of my life, however, it kept me fearful, limited, and stuck.

You see, it's really tough to move forward in life and improve when you're scared of disappointment. The only way we ever grow and do great things in life is when we are brave enough to dream bigger than who we are at any given moment. It would have taken bravery for me to go to that high school dance wanting to have a great time because it would have opened me up to the possibility of not having a great time. I'll never know what could have been if I did muster the courage to show up differently that night. Worst case scenario? The outcome wouldn't have been much different, but at least I would have tried.

You'll realize that living life without regrets means daring to show up, betting on yourself, and going for the gold, no matter the outcome. The actual result becomes far less important because you aren't discouraged by failure.

When I finally started to reprogram my brain, it felt like my world was slowly turning upside down. As I approached life with more bravery and positivity, little by little, I would find less evidence of the bad and more proof of the good. At first, I thought it was a fluke. Still, I continued to work on my new thought patterns, and one day it was like a lightbulb switched on. For the first time since childhood, I could appreciate the excitement and promise of life.

Take stock of how *you* approach life. Ask yourself these questions: "How often do you expect the worst from yourself or other people around you? How often do you assume negative things about the world or people around you (that are probably not true)? How often do you go into a situation waiting for the shoe to drop?"

In the following exercises, we'll identify some pesky thought patterns you have subconsciously programmed over the years and begin reprograming them into better ones.

EXERCISES

Establishing Positive Energy

Getting yourself into a more positive, peaceful, or energetic state is a helpful, if not necessary first step to rewiring your brain.

Changing our thought patterns becomes almost impossible if we continue to do the same things we've always done, follow the same routine, live with the same energy, and continue with the same habits. You can't rewire your brain from a place of stress, anxiety, or frustration. That's like training a dog to sit on top of hot asphalt. Doing an uplifting activity that puts you into a positive state will prime your brain for change.

What's that uplifting activity for you? For me, it's a few things: meditation, yoga, taking walks, playing with my dog, and listening to inspirational speeches.

Meditation is by far the easiest and most effective. In the age of instant communication and constant social media updates, making time to meditate for even five minutes a day requires discipline. However, it's probably the most helpful practice in shifting your energy, taking control of your thoughts, and rewiring your brain.

I suspect the reason people are so resistant to meditation is because they have this false notion that meditation requires you to totally silence your mind. That's impossible, and simply not true. Meditation is actually the practice of observing your thoughts but not getting caught up in them. When thoughts come in, accept them and let them pass.

If you're interested in starting a meditative practice, try it now! Wherever you're sitting, put this book down, close your eyes and begin to deepen your breath. Then scan your body from head to toe and focus on breathing into every part of your body. You can find many free guided meditations online that will walk you through a similar process. At the end of the meditation, you should feel relaxed and open. That's exactly the state we want to be in!

Whether meditation, yoga, sketching, or taking a walk, do something that shifts your energy into a more positive state for at least five to ten minutes, and then try the rewiring exercises below.

Identify the Negative Thoughts

To rewire your brain, you have to first be able to identify the thoughts that you want to rewire. This will require the self-awareness we've been developing in the earlier chapters.

Here's a question: Can you distance yourself from who you think you are?

Remember, like your feelings, your thoughts are not who you are. They don't define your value or your worth. As we've discovered earlier, most of our thoughts, according to the National Science Foundation, are negative! If we based our value on our thoughts alone, we'd all be a pretty big nervous wreck (like some of us are). That's precisely why we need to reprogram them.

The first step in identifying your thoughts is by, yes, you guessed it, writing them down. Only this time, I want you to convert those negative thoughts into belief statements.

So let's say some of your negative thoughts look like this:

- I'll never be popular, and it makes me feel bad.
- I'm not doing well in school, and it's frustrating.
- I'm not as talented as the other girls on the volleyball team.
- I don't have good social skills.
- People don't seem to like me very much.

Those thoughts would be distilled into simple, unemotional statements like the ones below:

- I'm not popular.
- I'm not smart.
- I'm not athletic.
- I'm not social.
- People don't like me.

When we begin to break down the negative thoughts we have throughout the day into simple beliefs, it's often pretty ugly. We would never say these things to our closest friends or family members, yet we let them roam around rent-free in our heads! It's a sad truth, but we are often the biggest bullies in our lives.

Rewiring the Brain Through Affirmations

Now, let's begin the rewiring. Positive affirmations are more than just some woo-woo concept to get you to believe delusional thoughts about yourself. They are a useful tool to help you chemically rewire the circuitry in your brain.

Think of it like learning a new dance routine. Let's say that every month since you were eleven years old, you put on the same dance routine for your parents using the same dance moves, over and over. By now, you have all the steps memorized like the back of your hand. You could practically do this dance routine in your sleep.

Then, suddenly, you're asked to do the same dance routine, only with several significant changes throughout the performance. It will take a lot of practice, repetition, and rehearsal to unlearn the previous moves and relearn the modified version.

At first, it will feel unnatural and uncomfortable and just plain weird because you've rehearsed the previous routine so many times for such a long time. You might even slip back into your old moves from time to time because that's what you were used to doing.

Creating positive affirmations for ourselves will help us rewire the brain by establishing new neural pathways, or new "routines," through repetition.

So take out the negative beliefs you wrote down in the previous exercise. On another paper, I want you to write objections to those beliefs, either by stating that you are enough without any change or by stating the opposite. Then I want you to add at the end "and I love and accept myself for where I am."

This would look like this:

- I'm as popular as I need to be, and I love and accept myself for where I am.
- I'm as smart as I need to be, and I love and accept myself for where I am.
- I'm as athletic as I need to be, and I love and accept myself for where I am.
- I can make new friends, and I love and accept myself for where I am.
- People do like me, and I love and accept myself for where I am.

When you have them all written down, I want you to repeat these last statements to yourself at least ten times while tapping on a part of your body, like we did in an earlier exercise. This can be on any meridian point we listed earlier: the side of your hand, below your clavicle, below your eyes, side of your eyes, below your nose, above your chin, top of your head, beneath your armpit. (Remember, you can do an online search of "the tapping method" to see this demonstrated)

You might feel an initial discomfort in your gut or stomach as you say these things because you're not used to talking to yourself this way, but that's precisely the point. We're in the process of creating new neural pathways in your brain that you rarely ever use, and it's going to feel weird. Bodybuilders don't go to the gym, hang out in the locker room and say: "I guess it's time to go home!" They build new muscles by putting their body through discomfort.

As a side note: isn't it sad that we find it so hard to say these simple, kind statements to ourselves out loud?

Also, please don't skip over the part "I love and accept myself for where I am." That's probably the most critical part of this whole rewiring exercise. As you'll see, genuinely accepting yourself for where you are right now and loving yourself unconditionally is the golden key to living a kickass life and achieving real empowerment. But that's for another time.

Repeat these statements to yourself ten times daily for the next ten days. At the end of those ten days, check in to see if anything inside of you has shifted.

Break Down the Program

Try this if you want to take positive affirmations to the next level.

When a negative thought pops up, whether that's a thought about a test, a grade, yourself, or a social interaction, write it down as a statement beginning with, "I've programmed myself to think…".

So it could look something like this:

- I've programmed myself to think I'm not smart enough to do well on my next math exam.
- I've programmed myself to believe I will be awkward at that dance.
- I've programmed myself to think I'll fail if I try to get better grades.
- I've programmed myself to believe that I am not likable.

The reason why it's important to write down your negative thoughts beginning with "I've programmed myself to think…" is because the vast majority of your negative thoughts are just that–programs that you've conditioned yourself to believe based on past experiences. I'm not saying there isn't room for improvement in your life, but what I *am* saying is that as long as you hold onto these negative thoughts as absolute truths, you completely shut yourself off from change.

Say you believe that you are always awkward at dances. You believe it so much that you don't think there is any other possible outcome when you go to a dance. Therefore, you avoid dances, never try to improve, and continue to solidify the false idea that you are always awkward at dances. Even if you've only ever been to two dances.

Do you see why that can become dangerous and unhelpful? When you start seeing your negative beliefs as programs, it gives you the power to *change* them.

Next, let's turn those negative beliefs on their heads. It would look something like:

- I am smart enough to do well on my next math exam.
- I'm going to be super social at that dance.
- If I try to get better grades, I'm going to succeed!
- I'm very likable.

Read the last statements and take stock of how they feel in your body. If it feels good, or even kind of good, that's great! You're already starting to break down your negative belief statements and replace them with new ones in your body.

Keep repeating these statements to yourself at least ten times everyday. Write them down where you can easily refer back to them, and repeat them for the next 30 days. Watch how your brain will shift to accommodate these new beliefs!

However, if those statements feel too forced or untrue, that can be counter-productive as it will create too much disbelief in your system and they won't have any energy behind them. Instead, try adding "It's possible" at the beginning of the statement. It could sound something like:

- It's possible for me to do well on my next math exam.
- It's possible for me to have a good time at the dance.
- It's possible that if I try, I can get better grades.
- It's possible that I'm likable.

Often adding "it's possible" at the beginning of a positive rewiring affirmation can make it feel more natural. Because the truth is, any of those things *can* be true. No matter how much your negative mind wants to argue with you, the fact is there are unlimited possibilities out there for you, you just have to believe that it's possible.

Practicing Thankfulness

You've probably heard this one, except it's more commonly called "practicing gratitude." I like to call it practicing thankfulness because "gratitude" can often be loaded with other feelings of shame or guilt. How often have you heard people say, "you should just be grateful for what you have"? Or even used it against you: "Why are you being so ungrateful?" Let's not enter that territory because it's neither helpful nor productive.

Practicing thankfulness is simply saying "thank you" for the things in your life that light you up–whether that's your best friend, parent, or the cool new journal you just bought (*wink wink*). What are the things in your life right now that, when you think about them, make you go, "Oh yeah, that's pretty awesome!"?

This isn't about forcing yourself to feel good about things that don't make you feel good. This is about taking stock of all the good that's already around you that we so easily overlook.

Remember, practicing thoughts we don't typically have is part of rewiring our brains. If you don't already reflect on all the great things in your life that make you feel good during the day, this exercise will help you see the positive around you everywhere you go.

What felt good? Every day for 30 days, before you go to sleep, write down or think about three things that you're thankful for from that day–whether it was an encounter with a kind teacher, a laugh session with your best friend, or even the fact that dinner was extra delicious. Once you get into the habit of practicing thankfulness, it will become a natural habit throughout the day.

By the way, practicing thankfulness has the added benefit of attracting more positive experiences into your life to be thankful for. From a physics perspective, everything is energy–your chair, your house, your phone, you. The great inventor Nikola Tesla once said, "If you want to know the secrets of the universe, think in terms of energy, frequency, and vibration." Haven't you ever said to someone, "that feels high vibe," or "that feels low vibe"? That's because you're actually picking up on the energy of that thing or person. Like-energy attracts like-energy, and when you live from a thankful energy state, you're more likely to attract experiences that reinforce that thankfulness.

You might not be able to snap your fingers and dissipate negative thoughts into thin air, but practicing these exercises regularly will help you develop that positivity muscle in your brain until, one day, "being positive" becomes part of who you are. Once you embrace the positive in yourself and the world around you, you will never look back.

Let me be upfront and say that rewiring your brain requires disciplined effort, and it's not a quick fix. One of the hardest things for me at the beginning of this process was pushing away judgmental thoughts about the process itself. Thoughts like "You're just being stupid," "This is pointless," or "This will never work" were trying to get me to give up. But like a bodybuilder who has to push beyond her limits when she hits a plateau, I had to force those thoughts aside and refocus on my bigger goal: living up to my potential.

Also, let me be clear that you *will* face negative thoughts no matter what. They are inevitable! Remember, at the beginning of this chapter, the goal was to shift an 80% negatively skewed mind into a 60% positively skewed one. When you reach a point where your thoughts are 60% positive, your whole life will change, and you won't even mind the 40%. This isn't about perfection—it's about improvement.

In the next chapter, we'll discuss one of the most important things to develop as you continue your journey toward empowerment: self-love.

8

DISCOVER SELF-LOVE

WHAT IS IT AND HOW TO CULTIVATE IT

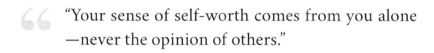 "Your sense of self-worth comes from you alone —never the opinion of others."

— ROBERT GREENE

You might want to roll your eyes when you hear "self-love." I know I did. Until my mid-twenties, I thought "self-love" was some silly concept that only existed to make people feel better about themselves. "I don't need more self-love. I need to be popular, thinner, and prettier, and *then* I'll give myself some self-love!" I told myself. Unfortunately, I wouldn't discover this until much later in life, but I had it *entirely* backward.

Let's first get on the same page, though. What is real "self-love," anyway? And what does it look like? Does it mean sending myself flowers and telling myself how amazing I am? Does it mean having a healthy diet? Does it mean speaking up for myself? Does it mean taking baths every day?

Self-love can look like all those things, but it doesn't have to.

True self-love is knowing who you are and knowing you are enough. It's trying hard, failing, and getting back up again. It's forgiving yourself for all the shame and embarrassment you've felt in the past. It's appreciating every aspect of who you are now, even if you know there are some things you'd like to improve. It's never letting other people's opinions of you dictate how you feel about yourself. It's taking care of yourself before others. It's never giving up on yourself–whether that means pursuing a goal, being happy, or being the best version of yourself every day. It's an unshakeable knowing that even if everything else in your life crumbled, your value would remain intact.

Developing self-love is one critical aspect that I overlooked for years. If someone had told me that creating a sense of deep self-love would be the secret to unlocking everything good in life, I would have saved myself years of pain. It took a lot of struggle and loss to finally come to terms with its importance, and when I did, it changed everything. My relationships, career, confidence, and happiness all started to come into me in a new way.

Before we go further, we need to really understand the mechanics behind self-love.

"Self-love," in my experience, is the natural byproduct of having a "sense of self." Once you define your sense of self, it's natural to lean into self-love because you know who you are, and you can finally see how amazing that person is!

When I was in high school, I really liked this guy. He was one of the funniest people in my class, and I had a thing for funny men (I still do). But I was so unable to deal with my huge crush for him that I'd end up sitting at lunch staring at him while gnawing on my egg salad sandwich.

One day, he called me out on it. Yes. There I was, sitting on the quad with my mini bag of Lay's potato chips, daydreaming, thinking, "He's so cute." Suddenly, he turns, points at me, and yells, "Hey, I see you staring at me, weirdo!" Everyone turned to me, and my face lit up brighter than Rudolph's nose. The following week I felt so embarrassed; all I wanted to do was crawl into a hole and disappear. "My life is over," I thought.

Now, before you start feeling too bad for me, I married an incredible man who is miles funnier than anyone I ever had a crush on during my high school days. Yes, dreams do come true.

But of course I couldn't have known that then, and in that moment, my world shattered. How was I ever going to get over such humiliation?

It's a real possibility that you get into social situations where you feel helpless, embarrassed, and ashamed, and that's okay. That's part of this whole thing we signed up for: the human experience.

I hate to break the news to you, but even in adult years, it's still possible to face humiliation. Online bullying, public criticism, and embarrassment *can* happen, especially if you put yourself out there in life. It's impossible to avoid negative feedback unless you lock yourself up in a basement, never go anywhere, and never do anything. But then, are you really living?

I can't tell you how many people I know who are a few decades out of school and still worry about their image on social media. They still fear getting negative comments and criticism online from total strangers. These worries and fears of what *might* happen literally prevent them from being seen and heard in all of their brilliance and glory.

Let's think logically for a moment. Suppose we can't avoid unpleasant situations because they will always happen in some way or another. In that case, the only thing we *can* do is become more resilient to them. A duck isn't worried about a rainy day because it has water-resistant feathers that protect it from getting wet.

So, we should ask the real question: "What's the human equivalent of water-resistant feathers?"

Developing a solid sense of self.

A strong sense of self is knowing who you are at your core. It has nothing to do with what you look like, your clothes, your car, your house, your grades, or your friends. When you start to live from a strong sense of self, you begin to have a greater acceptance of who you are, which is not defined by anything outside you because you define yourself! When you embody this way of living, you have no choice but to exist in a state of self-love.

Let's go back to my humiliating lunch story. If I had built a strong sense of self, I might have still turned bright red from embarrassment, but the recovery period would have been much shorter, and shrugging it off over the next day or two, would have been much more manageable. As for the guy? I would have asked myself, "Why am I so into a guy who doesn't seem to be a very nice person? Don't I deserve better?"

Do you see how developing a strong sense of self is one of the most powerful things you can cultivate in life?

Think of someone, anyone who has achieved greatness. I guarantee you there were plenty of reasons for them to give up or make excuses before reaching their success. I'm sure they faced criticism, failure, ridicule, rejection, hardship, and embarrassment. Yet, they persevered because, deep down, they knew that giving up on themselves was a much worse offense than making a mistake, being laughed at, or failing. They learned how to become that duck with water-resistant feathers.

Let's take some prominent examples. Lady Gaga, Michael Jordan, Michael Jackson, Madonna, Elton John. No one would call these people small, self-deprecating, or withdrawn. Yet, I'm pretty sure they received a ton of criticism, rejection, and even ridicule from the people around them before reaching the kind of success they did. If they didn't have that voice inside them saying: "This is who I am, and I deserve it," do you think they would have gotten as far as they did in life? As the saying goes, "Fortune favors the bold."

In life, it's easy to stumble, and there will always be people and situations that will highlight your stumbles and make you feel small or weird, or wrong. But ultimately, it's up to you to make the final call about how you want to see yourself.

Until recently, I had difficulty knowing who I was without outside input from others. Whenever I made a decision, I had to consult with multiple people. On the rare occasion I made my own decision, I would get so lost in examining it from other people's eyes: *How would my friends feel about me wearing this shirt? Will people think I'm trying too hard? I like this dress, but I don't know if other people will. What will my parents think?*

Almost all of my decisions in life throughout my teens and twenties were based on how I thought other people would feel about them. I usually had an idea of what I wanted, but as soon as I received an outside opinion about the "smartest" or the "safest" or the "most secure" thing to do, I wasn't sure anymore. My weak sense of self made it challenging to commit to anything for any period because I never felt like my decisions were entirely mine! And when I did commit to something, it was usually for the wrong reasons, which never ended well.

I stayed in relationships far longer than I should have because other people thought it was the "right" thing to do. I stayed at jobs longer than I wanted because it was the "safe" thing to do. When I made a decision for myself, I couldn't move forward confidently because I always relied on other people's feedback to cheer me on.

What happens when you have a weak sense of self is you succumb easily to the opinions of others and tend to make decisions that are not your own. This makes you vulnerable to peer pressure, brainwashing and following the crowd because "other people are doing it" even when it doesn't make sense for your situation. You become a leaf floating downstream, a passenger of your own life. At some point, you might stop, turn around and ask: "How did I get here? Was this what I really wanted?" This is what many people call a "mid-life crisis."

Here are some additional benefits to developing a strong sense of self:

- People can trust you because you are clear about your values and who you are.

- You don't sacrifice your own happiness for the sake of others.
- You don't succumb to peer pressure.
- You are more open to developing new skills because you aren't discouraged by failure.
- Negative people don't stop you from your goals.
- You are more willing to put yourself out there and be authentic.
- You live life with less regret.

When you develop a strong sense of self, you finally appreciate that you are your own best friend, mentor, ally, motivator, and driver. You carry a deep knowing that no matter what happens around you, or even to you, you and only you hold power over your life.

So how do you know if you have a strong sense of self?

1. You can make your own decisions without needing other people's approval. When you face a different opinion, you still remain comfortable with your choices. (this isn't to say that you can't consult with people for their advice, but after getting advice, you know your decision is yours alone)
2. You are your own biggest supporter. You don't let other people dictate how you see yourself. If someone gives you a critical comment, you can listen to it without it negatively impacting your sense of self-worth.

3. You are consistent. Whether with your parents, friends, or crush, you are consistent with your values, principles, and perspectives. You don't try to change who you are to accommodate those around you because you don't need anyone else's approval to define you.

If you identified with all three statements, congratulations! You have a strong sense of self!

If your answers were a "maybe" or a "no," that means you haven't yet cultivated a strong sense of self, which is totally okay. As I mentioned before, most people never get there. Or maybe they end up having a mid-life crisis that forces them there. But thankfully, we can prevent that from happening, and that's why you're reading this book.

The following exercises are designed to help you understand what it actually feels like to have a solid sense of self so you can begin to define it.

EXERCISES

Golden Column Visualization

Sit up straight in a chair, on your bed, anywhere. Close your eyes. Imagine a glowing golden column running from the bottom of your tailbone to the top of your head. Imagine it glowing with your whole life force. Maybe it makes a sound; maybe it's silent. Maybe it feels warm, or maybe it feels cold. But it gets brighter and brighter, and the brighter it gets, the more it strengthens. Repeat the following words to yourself: "This is who I am. Nothing and no one can violate that."

By creating this visual in your body and saying the words, you are tapping into your sense of self, which is not defined by your looks, grades, talent, house, or partner. It is defined by you and only you. If you want to change the words to something that feels more powerful for you, do it.

You might not feel anything the first few times you do this exercise. You might be in your head. Keep with it. Keep imagining that golden column getting stronger and stronger.

You'll likely have resistance to this exercise. "What good is it to imagine some stupid column that's not even there? What am I, five?"

When you think about it, everything starts in your head. From planning your outfits to deciding who you'll sit with at lunch, many of your decisions go through your imagination before you even act on them. In the book *7 Habits of Highly Effective People*, Dr. Stephen R. Covey states that all things are created twice. First in the imagination and then in the real world. Just as buildings are physically built from drawn-up blueprints (which, again, are imagined from the mind), our actions follow our imaginations.

A Harvard Medical School experiment proved that imagination has an actual physical effect on our bodies. They measured two groups of people. The first group was told to practice a five-finger piano exercise for two hours daily over five days. The second group was instructed to practice the five-finger piano exercise, but only in their imaginations (no finger movement). After a week, the part of the brain that deals with finger movements expanded the same way in both groups.

This golden column exercise is powerful because it strengthens your focus on your internal state rather than anything outside you. It allows you to feel the power and strength that you can generate in your body. As you feel that golden column growing in your spine, that's literally the sensation of your sense of self wanting to beam through you.

I still use this exercise. For example, suppose I receive a negative text, or someone is being extra salty with me. I take a second to stop and imagine the golden column in my spine and let everything else just mentally "fall away."

Next time you're in a tense social situation, or nervous about a particular event, try it. Sit up straight, and imagine that golden column glowing up and down your spine. Remember that anything outside that column does not affect or define you–and let the rest fall away in your mind's eye.

Take the Bird's Eye Perspective

When you feel like you're losing yourself, physically elevate your perspective to look down on the situation from a bird's eye view.

When we're "in it," it's tough for us to view things objectively. Therefore, it's much easier to "lose" ourselves in the current situation. When I was younger, the magnitude of everything felt like life or death. My crush humiliating me. Getting a bad grade on a paper. My friend moving to another school. That nasty comment made by a peer. It all felt so dramatic, and I became that wayward leaf floating downstream, just hoping for a smooth ride.

Next time you're starting to feel insecure or anxious, try placing your awareness above your current situation. In other words, pretend like you're a bird that's flying high above yourself, looking down on the situation. How do things feel from that perspective? Is it as scary or as stressful as you initially thought? Does this situation define who you are in the grand scheme of things? Will you even care about this in a month or even next week?

When I'd get a negative comment on social media, it used to feel like a punch in the gut. The thoughts, "Oh no! How could they??" or "Am I really that bad?" would take over my thoughts for hours, sometimes even days. Then I started to use this technique.

I looked down at myself from overhead. I could see myself lying on the bed, staring at my phone. I could see my reaction to the comment and felt how insignificant the event really was in the grand scheme of my life. I came back down and put the comment into proper perspective. "Hm, it's really not as life-altering as I made it out to be," I thought. Okay, next.

When you're in that mode, it's also easier to address why you're feeling what you're feeling and practice more profound levels of self-awareness. It could go something like "What a stupid, ignorant person! They're awful!" to "I feel embarrassed that someone doesn't like my post," to "It hurts to have someone not like my post because it makes me feel like I'm not good enough," to "I'm worried I'm not good enough."

When you boil thoughts and reactions down to core limiting beliefs, you can use that information to apply those rewiring exercises we learned in the previous chapter. Maybe instead of "I'm not good enough," the new belief could be: "I'm as good as I need to be, and I love and accept myself for where I am."

Owning Yourself

This next exercise is another mental rewiring practice, and a fun one!

I want you to write down some qualities that other people like, love, admire, or respect about you. It could go something like:

- People like my fun personality
- People respect my work ethic.
- People admire the fact that I'm good at math.
- People love my taste in music.
- People admire that I'm good at drawing.

Now, I want you to do something kind of unconventional. At the end of those qualities, I want you to add, "but even if this weren't true, I'm still kickass and deserve to love, respect, and honor myself."

So that would look something like this:

- People like my fun personality, but even if this weren't true, I'm still kickass and deserve to love, respect, and honor myself.
- People respect my work ethic, but even if this weren't true, I'm still kickass and deserve to love, respect, and honor myself.
- People admire the fact that I'm good at math, but even if this weren't true, I'm still kickass and deserve to love, respect, and honor myself.
- People love my taste in music, but even if this weren't true, I'm still kickass and deserve to love, respect, and honor myself.
- People admire that I'm good at drawing, but even if this weren't true, I'm still kickass and deserve to love, respect and honor myself.

I want you to repeat these out loud, and when you say them, I want you to give them some extra juice and repeat them like you *truly* mean it. Like you're going to convince the whole world that they're true! Try walking around your room while doing it! The more energy you can give it, the more powerful it will be.

Once you're done, you should feel a kind of buzzing in your body, almost like a high. And if you pay close attention, you might even feel this internal strength growing within you. That's your sense of self.

This exercise might initially feel counterintuitive, so let me explain. So often, we tie our value or sense of worth to "positive" traits that others perceive in us. While those qualities can be valuable, they still don't define your value as a person. It's important to remember this because as much as we don't want to become prisoners to our limiting beliefs, we also don't want to become prisoners to the qualities that others have defined for us.

For example, let's say you're known to be generous with your time and energy. This can be seen as an admirable quality to others, but what if it doesn't serve you to give away your time and energy so freely? What if you should reserve time and energy for yourself so you can work on a passion or give yourself some self-care? If you define your value as being a generous person to others, it would be tough to put yourself first in a time of personal need.

Do you see how we can become prisoners to our "positive" qualities if we don't have a strong sense of self?

When you finally recognize that the only person who can determine your worth is you, you will be much harder pressed to give it away to anyone else. Yes, even if your crush calls you out for staring at him in the middle of the quad at lunch. You're going to take a second and think: "Yeah, but is it really worth letting this ruin my week and selling myself short?" The answer is probably "no." At the end of the day, you have to hold your value to the highest standards because you're worthy of it.

The next chapter is going to be a fun one. We are going to define your hero's journey so that you can begin walking that path. Since you're the main character of your life, let's start claiming that energy.

9

YOUR HERO'S JOURNEY

AWAKEN THE HERO INSIDE OF YOU

> "It is during the hard times when the 'hero' within us is revealed."

— BOB RILEY

You are your greatest hero in life. It may sound cheesy, but it's true. After all, why are the same cheesy superhero tropes so popular? It's because deep down we recognize the deeper truths in those cheesy tropes. We can all relate to the universal themes of courage, self-belief, and heroism, because it's hardwired into our DNA.

We love a flawed protagonist. We love that despite their superhuman strength, deep down, they're humans, just like us. We love that they have deep wounds that they try to bury and avoid, just like us. And we love that when they're finally forced to face their demons, they rise to the challenge and summon the courage to overcome them, just like us. That's the blueprint of a good hero movie because that's the blueprint of our lives.

We may not have spidey senses or lightning speed, but we all have our own hero's journey. Yes, even you. We are all born with unique circumstances, gifts, blind spots, challenges, and desires. And these unique qualities give us the story arc that will define the larger journey of our lives.

So how do you find *your* arc?

Earlier in this book, you used your self-awareness to discover some limiting beliefs. You observed, dissected, and created affirmations to help you rewire your brain around them. But how do you get the grit to actually apply what you've learned when you're feeling at your worst, and you just want to wallow in a pool of self-pity? How do you summon that extra courage to continue forward, stronger than ever?

From my experience, giving someone an exercise or two might help. Still, a more significant purpose has to glue those pieces together. Otherwise, we fail to see the bigger "point." We go to high school because we think that once we get our high school diploma, we can apply for jobs, build a career, and move forward with life. Without it, we can't do those things effectively (or so we've been told). So, what's that diploma for being your best self? What's going to keep you focused on the prize?

I've always loved movies, especially romantic comedies with flawed leading ladies. One of my favorites is "Bridget Jones's Diary" (yes, I'm dating myself). It's a film about a depressed, awkward, struggling woman with a gold heart who, through stumbles, mishaps, and embarrassments, rises from the ashes and finds confidence and love. And most importantly, she finds acceptance in herself.

That movie was close to my heart because it made me see that it was okay to be flawed and socially awkward. It was okay sometimes to find myself in a rut. It was okay to stumble in life and ultimately find my way through it because somewhere in me, I knew I deserved better. Despite the number of times I struggled, I could still be the leading lady of my own life and hold my head high. Yes, even when my crush humiliated me on the lunch quad, I could still love myself and be loved.

When I was in high school, all I wanted deep down was to be acknowledged for being worthy in whatever way that looked like–being pretty, smart, liked, respected, or trendy. I thought that if I dressed, looked, and acted the part, it would be easy to shine and show everyone how genuinely confident I was!

If someone at the time told me that none of those things would have actually solved my low-self worth, I would have rolled my eyes and said, "Yeah, well, it's easy for you to say! You're not me!" and "Is that what you tell all the other girls who *do* have those things?" and "How do you know?" It would have been hard to believe because I would have looked at other girls who had everything and thought, "How unlucky was I to be born me instead of her?"

My biggest mistake in my twenties was trying to cover up my lack of confidence with things and achievements. "Once I make this much money," or "Once I lose this amount of weight," or "Once I date this kind of partner," and the list went on and on. Even when I would attain those things, they left me empty because I was still plagued with that profound lack of self-worth.

The reality was I could have made a billion dollars, married the man of my dreams, and achieved the perfect body, and I'd still be scratching my head, thinking, "I'm still not confident. What now?" You see, when you feed a problem with the wrong answer, no matter how many wrong answers you come up with, it will always be the wrong answer.

In life's cruel irony, when I finally stopped relying on outside things to give me confidence, I actually began to find it. Like Superman finally willing to confront his kryptonite and brave Lex Luther's den without his superpowers, I had to be willing to take a hard look at myself and ask the difficult question: "Why can't I feel worthy without all these things?"

I eventually had to face the biggest question of them all: "Can I love myself for where I am right now?" The honest answer, at the time, was "No." I couldn't find reasons to love myself because I didn't know what loving myself even meant. I had taken on so many negative beliefs over the years that I was unable to give myself permission to feel good about just being me.

That's when I knew there was something very wrong. It took me losing everything I had at the time—a boyfriend, money, and my health to finally sit down and rebuild my sense of self on my own terms. I knew I had to let go of who I thought I was, in order to evolve into who I would become. It wasn't always a fun process.

I began to uncover those negative beliefs that I had held inside of me for years. Then I began to rewire those negative beliefs into positive ones. Then, little by little, I began to make other minor changes in my life. As I committed myself to the process more and more, I realized that the antidote to my lack of self-confidence wasn't in achieving more things but in healing myself from the inside out. Over time, I felt myself becoming happier and more confident.

So what underlying beliefs prevent you from feeling confident, accepted, and happy? What makes you say: "If only I had X, I'd be able to be X?" Is it your friends, your looks, your house, your clothes? Or maybe once you have good grades, you'd finally feel accomplished. Or maybe once you have that boyfriend, you'll finally be able to feel good about yourself.

The previous statements might feel convincing, but basing your value on anything that can be taken from you is a losing game. What if you wore the hottest trends, now...from the '80s? Exactly. Because inevitably, things, people, jobs, ideas, possessions, and even thoughts change, but the one thing that stays constant in your life is you. When you stake your value on anything outside your inherent internal value, you're eventually forced to deal with its fragility.

When I lost my boyfriend, my success, and my security in my early twenties, my world came crashing down on me because I had built my entire self-worth on having those things! I didn't know it at the time, but it was the wake-up call I needed to force me to look at the dark parts of myself— my limiting beliefs, my low self-worth, the reasons why I felt like I needed more "things" to make myself feel valuable at all.

In retrospect, I wish I had the self-awareness and the courage to face my low self-worth sooner. I wish I would have put my inside needs first instead of hiding behind external things. I wish I would have saved myself from the unnecessary anxiety and stress of worrying about things that ultimately wouldn't make me a better or happier person.

When I finally had the bravery to heal myself from the inside out, I reached a place where: I had desires, but I didn't need them to make me happy. I had goals, but not at the sacrifice of my health. I had dreams, but the biggest one was just becoming the healthiest, happiest, and best version of myself possible.

I won't claim I'm the most confident person you'll ever meet, but I've come a long way. I try at the things I love, embrace change, and commit myself to growth every single day. I know that my value goes beyond anything tangible or material and that knowledge is priceless. One more thing: people never tell me that I'm lacking in confidence. In fact, people come to me to help them find theirs!

I'm telling you—when you're finally willing to do the internal work and address those limiting beliefs that hold you down, the freedom you unlock within yourself will make you feel like a new person! You can enjoy life in a way that popularity, clothes, or fame can never give you. You will pursue your interests and desires with more enthusiasm and confidence. And you'll have a deep knowing that, in the end, you'll be all right. The tangible results are often so much better, too.

If I were to define my hero's journey, it would be something like this: An awkward, unconfident girl wishes to be accepted by her peers but never feels good enough. She snags a boyfriend, achieves some success, loses weight—does everything in her power to find acceptance and happiness, but nothing works. As a last resort, she focuses her attention inward, and there, she discovers her real purpose was never to find acceptance from her peers but to find acceptance within herself. From that moment on, she would make it her bigger life's mission to empower others to do the same.

By focusing my attention away from the external and to the internal, I was able to rewire my beliefs so that I could finally see my real value. It might not sound like an exciting or cool process, but at the end of the day, isn't that what every great superhero movie is about? The protagonist finally realizes that their ultimate strength isn't in their powers but in their courage to look within. The same is true for you.

The reason it's important to explore your hero's journey is because it empowers you to discover what every protagonist in every movie has to realize at the end of the day–that you and only you determine your fate and destiny.

You have the potential to be that radiant being you were when you were a child, but it's your decision to walk the path to get there. I don't know what that journey will look like for you, but I know that it's one worth taking as soon as possible. Inside of you is a story and an arch that will take you from insecure to undeniably worthy.

So what beliefs are holding you back? Do you still think you need better grades to feel deserving? Or more popular friends to feel confident? Or the latest makeup trends to feel worthy? What about the million followers? Maybe you still believe that your value lies somewhere outside of you.

In the following exercises, we'll leverage some of your current negative beliefs to propel you closer toward your brilliant self.

EXERCISES

Feel the Hero Within

We briefly touched on limiting self-beliefs in an earlier chapter. Here, we'll cover it again, on a deeper level. If you commit yourself to just *one* exercise in this book, this would be it!

Let's look at some negative beliefs you might currently hold about yourself.

Here's an example:

- I'm not likable
- I'm not pretty
- I'm not cool
- I'm not smart

Now, let's break down WHY you need to be any of those things. It might come down to something like this:

- I want to be likable so that I can have a lot of friends...
- I want to be pretty so that people will finally see me...

- I want to be cool so I can feel good about myself with other people...
- I want to be smart so that I can get into a good college...

Continue asking the question WHY you need to have a lot of friends or why you need people to finally see you, and you'll probably, in the end, come down to something like this...

- I want to be likable so that I can have a lot of friends...so that I can feel worthy.
- I want to be pretty so that people will finally see me...so that I can feel worthy.
- I want to be cool so that I can feel good about myself with other people...so that I can feel worthy.
- I want to be smart so that I can get into a good college...so that I can feel worthy.

I think you get the picture. Many of our insecurities, if not all, really boil down to one of our biggest and most commonly held beliefs about ourselves: that we are not worthy.

And as you know, feeding the wrong solution to a problem won't fix the problem. So we need to start fixing the problem, which is believing that we aren't worthy, deserving, or valuable. Because we are. We were born into this world fully worthy of becoming the hero of our lives.

Now, I want you to start your initial beliefs with "I don't need to be…" and end the statement with "to be the powerful hero of my life."

- I don't need to be likable to be the powerful hero of my own life.
- I don't need to be pretty to be the powerful hero of my life.
- I don't need to be cool to be the powerful hero of my life.
- I don't need to be smart to be the powerful hero of my life.

Repeat these to yourself five times, with the same resolve that a superhero would have when she decides to finally defeat the villain.

Do you feel how that shifts your energy? That's called a sense of empowerment. That's called a sense of self-worth. Whether you believe it or not, the statements you just read are true. No matter what you accumulate in your life—a partner, good grades, popularity, a career— those things do *not* make you the powerful hero of *your* life. You do.

I hope one day you can fully understand that. I hope it can start here.

Discover your Hero's Journey

I want you to start writing down what *your* hero's journey might look like. This will require some of that imagination you had as a kid and a lot of honesty and self-awareness. So, get out your pen and paper and answer the following questions:

1. Who are you right now? If you were the lead in your own movie, how would you describe your character at the beginning of the film (good and bad traits)?
2. At the film's end, who is the person you imagine that character would become?
3. What qualities, actions, or traits would that character need to develop to go from the person at the beginning of the movie to the person at the end?

Take your time with this exercise and think about your answers and what feels authentic and genuine to you. Make sure it's not based on a specific desired outcome like having a boyfriend or being popular. It should be based on the qualities and values of a person you might admire in a film.

If I were to have done this exercise, it would have looked something like this:

1. Paget is an awkward girl who gets teased by her classmates, but deep down, there's a soulful strength inside of her that knows she has more to offer. She tries to fit in, but nothing seems to work, and she hides behind her textbooks to avoid attention.

2. Paget has become a confident, go-getter who doesn't let the opinions of her peers deter her from being her authentic self (even if that *is* a little awkward at times). She never shies away from a challenge. She shows others that it's okay to be who they are, even if it's not perfect, as long as they love themselves.

3. She would not care about what other people think of her. She would be sure about who she is and would not try to conform to what others want her to be. She wouldn't place importance on trends or social status.

Now, unlike the movies, going from the character at the beginning of the movie to the character at the film's end is not going to be an overnight process. Growth takes time and effort, and this journey will be lifelong.

However, this exercise allows you to imagine a more fantastic version of yourself that one day, you will become. Just know that whatever you write down is possible.

Practicing Your Hero Self

This is similar to an earlier exercise where I asked you to document events in your life like a researcher, except this version has a bit of a twist.

Not only will you document the events that took place, but you're also going to report on them from a third-party perspective, like a book's narrator. Then comes a fun twist.

For instance, if I were to have done this exercise with the embarrassing lunch example, it would have sounded something like this:

He pointed at her and said, "I see you staring at me, weirdo!" At that moment, she felt a massive wave of embarrassment. She could barely breathe. Her face turned red and hot, and all she wanted to do was disappear....."

This is where the twist comes in. At a critical point during your narration, you're going to state what the hero version of you would have done in the same situation. It might continue something like this:

"But then she realized the guy she had a crush on was just a mean person. She stood up, looked him in the eye, and said: "Actually, I was just admiring how ugly you are on the inside." She turned and walked away.

Let me emphasize that this version of events never happened because I wasn't ready to step into that hero version of myself at that point in my life. You might not be ready to do that, either, and that's totally okay! Just know that that person exists within you, and every time you do this exercise, you will start to incorporate this person into your life, little by little.

In reality, your everyday progress might look like this: You decide to raise your hand in class and volunteer to go first.

You go over and introduce yourself to the new kid in class. You stand up for another student when he is being picked on. You become the bigger person in an argument with your friend and apologize first.

I don't know what those steps will look like for you, but growing into the hero of your life will take time and practice, so be patient with yourself. As long as you know that the hero version of you is just waiting to be unleashed, that gap between who you are and who you will become will start to close.

In fact, if you practice this exercise regularly enough, at some point, you will automatically ask yourself throughout the day: "How *would* the best version of myself handle this? How *would* the hero version of myself react in this situation?"

None of us can be the superheroes we see in the movies, but we can be something even greater–the hero we can always rely on. The person who will push us to be better every single day. The person who will forgive and show us compassion for during our tough times. And the person who will always rise to the challenge.

In the next chapter, we will explore one of the most important steps in truly becoming the empowered version of you. That's stepping outside of your comfort zone.

10

STEP OUTSIDE OF YOUR COMFORT ZONE

HOW TO PUT YOUR HERO INTO ACTION

> *"Losers quit when they fail. Winners fail until they succeed."*
>
> — *ROBERT T. KIYOSAKI*

L ike all heroes, you can never achieve greatness without stepping outside of your comfort zone. Think about it. If you watched a movie where the main protagonist never challenged herself, never changed, and never grew, would you really want to watch that movie? The same idea applies to life.

Our current challenges in life don't determine who we are; it's how we face those unique challenges that define who we will become. As cliché as it sounds, challenge makes us stronger, more skillful, dynamic, capable, and resilient. If we never faced any difficulties in life, we'd be the same people we were when we were born.

If Peter Parker didn't challenge himself to start using his powers for good, he wouldn't be Spiderman. He'd just be some kid who was given incredible powers for no reason whatsoever. If he had never asked MJ to go out with him, he would have never won the girl of his dreams. That would make for a pretty unexciting superhero movie.

So it's time for you to step into your role as the main character of your own life. What would you do if you were the hero in your own movie? Would you shy away from swinging the bat or would you step up to the plate with your knees shaking? Would you care more about what other people thought of you or live by your own values?

Rising to challenge doesn't require being "special" or uniquely brave. We all admire bravery because it's an inherent quality that lives inside us. Yes, even *you*. When you were born, you were pretty much inadequate at everything. Yet, you decided to take on new challenges and learn things like walking, talking and socializing. When babies witness people strolling across the room, they think, "If they can do it, I can, too." And that's the attitude of someone with a healthy dose of self-esteem.

We were all born with a good amount of self-esteem, but sometime between our toddler and teen years, we started to doubt ourselves. We thought that somehow we were the exception and maybe we weren't so brilliant. We slipped into self-deprecating thoughts like, "She's social and can make friends easily, but not me." "She can study and get an A on that test, but I can't." Have you stopped to think that you're not the exception? That pretty much anything anyone is capable of doing is something that you were, or are capable of, too?

Sound like too much of a stretch? What about Jacky Hunt-Broersma, a woman with one leg who ran 104 marathons in 104 days? Or Cornel Hrisca-Munn, a man without forearms who has become a world-class drummer? Or Jeff Hansen, a renowned painter who lost his eyesight as a child?

You've probably never heard of these people, and that's the point. These everyday people are doing extraordinary things that go so far beyond any conventional expectation set out for them. So how did they do it? How did they rise to the challenge and beat all odds? Firstly, by choosing not to let the challenges they faced create limitations in their lives.

This isn't to say some people aren't born with talent, but I guarantee you those talents were cultivated with conscious effort, time, and practice so that they *could* become a great runner, they *could* become a world-class drummer, or they *could* be the next Monet. The perceived gap between you and anyone else in this world lies primarily in self-belief, effort, and the ability to take on discomfort.

I'm not a natural academic. In fact, growing up, my teachers would take my parents aside and ask them if I spoke another language at home (I did not) because I was constantly staring out the window and daydreaming. I also hated reading and couldn't stand doing homework. My older sister, on the other hand, loved reading books. She would lock herself in her room and read for hours while I watched cartoons and sketched pictures of unicorns.

For the longest time, I wasn't interested in excelling in school. I was too preoccupied with drawing and daydreaming to concern myself with a teacher's curriculum. It wasn't until middle school when I saw how hard my older sister worked to get good grades, that I decided I wanted to do the same.

Now, admittedly, I had an advantage. My sister lived in the same household as me, and we had the same genes, so I *knew* that if I wanted to, I could get good grades, too. In my mind, there wasn't anything stopping me besides application. So I started to apply myself. I spent hours on homework and asked for teacher's assistance after school–I did everything I could to get good grades, even though it didn't feel "natural" to me.

Because I established in my head that I could do it, I worked my butt off for four years and eventually graduated valedictorian (something even my sister didn't do). To this day, I still maintain that she's more academic and naturally more intelligent than I ever was. Not only were her SAT scores well above mine, but her IQ, as we found out, was significantly higher.

As you get older, you see that what matters in life is not the fortune or talent you were born into. What truly matters and defines your level of empowerment is your willingness to be a better version of yourself every day–in whatever way that looks.

First, you have to know that you are not set in stone. You *can* change, and inevitably, you *do* change. Unfortunately, most people leave it up to life's circumstances to force them into change (and often not for the better), but what if you started to take your development into your own hands? What if you decided today that you would muster up the bravery and willingness to step outside of your comfort zone and start being that hero?

Getting straight A's wasn't as easy as deciding to do it. Sometimes I felt sluggish and didn't want to put in the extra effort to finish that paper. Sometimes I worked my butt off studying for a test, only to get a lower grade than people who didn't work as hard. Did it hurt? Yes. Was it discouraging? Sure. I'd wallow for a few hours, or even a day or two, but at the end of the day, I was still focused on my goal.

What's that goal for you? For me, it was getting good grades. For you, it could be getting on the cross-country team, playing in a band, or creating cool content online. The goal itself doesn't really matter. The bigger picture is being able to set your sights on a target and commit to the effort, despite the discomfort.

I'm proud that I was valedictorian, not because I think the title has much value, but because I stretched myself beyond my limits. Even though it wasn't easy, I had the self-esteem to go after it.

I have to mention that there's a difference between wanting to achieve something because you know you are worthy of it and wanting to achieve something because you're trying to prove you are worthy of it. Too often, I see people set big goals for themselves because they are trying to make up for something they lack on the inside. Not only do these people tend to give up pretty quickly (remember my college example?), but if they ever do reach their goal, it ends up feeling hollow and meaningless.

So what if you flip the switch? What if you begin knowing how worthy, valuable, and unique you are, and then you set a goal because you know without a doubt that you deserve to achieve it?

Instead of: "I don't feel good about myself. Maybe if I had more friends, I'd feel better. I need to do whatever it takes to make people like me!"

You'd say to yourself: "I'm valuable and worthy right now, but I'd like to work on my ability to meet new people. Not only is it a great skill to have, but it's something I think I'd enjoy."

Do you see the difference? It sounds like a small shift, but it's actually huge. Instead of being desperate for results to prove something to yourself and others, you work toward results because you enjoy the process of growing.

Now I know all of this "willingness to grow" stuff might sound a little cheesy, but there's truth in cheesy. Who doesn't love seeing the underdog make a comeback? Or hear a heartfelt story about the power of love? Or watch a stone-cold villain transform into the hero with a heart of gold?

Why are we moved when we watch a movie where the meek protagonist finally decides to speak up for herself? Was it because it was easy for her? No, it's because, at that moment, she doubled down on herself. She said, "I'm going to risk what I have because I know that my value is worth more than anything I could lose." And in that moment of bravery, our protagonist found her true confidence.

So you might be wondering—if I feel so great and valuable, why would I need to step outside my comfort zone? Why would I need to better myself?

The funny thing about developing true confidence is that you are more willing to try new things, put in the effort to learn new skills, and want to better yourself in many different ways because you "deserve" it. Having self-worth doesn't mean you can't improve; it just means the outcome doesn't define you.

Remember that baby at the beginning of this chapter? Well, some odd years ago, that was you! At that time, you had no reason to think you were less valuable or worthy than anyone else on the planet, yet you wanted to learn new things. In fact, you were ready and willing to fall down hundreds of times before you finally learned how to walk on your own. After that, you learned how to speak, write, and tie your shoes. Evolution and improvement were natural processes of your being.

So let's explore ways you can evolve. What would you like to improve on? Is it your ability to meet new people? Public speaking? Sports? Music? What's something that you'd like to develop in yourself that feels challenging, inspiring, and worth the effort?

Maybe for you, it's being more outgoing and socializing. Maybe it's trying out for the cheerleading squad or choir. Maybe it's auditioning for that school play. Maybe it's trying out for the soccer team. It's likely the first thing that popped into your head when you read the question.

You might not be able to tackle it today, tomorrow, or even the next day, but first and foremost, you have to be willing to admit what it is you actually want. Sometimes it's hard to admit what we want because it feels like we're admitting some kind of vulnerability, which is not seen as "cool."

The problem with living in "cool" mode is that we'll never be willing to try anything new because the learning phase is, simply put, never a "cool" process. Unlike the Marvel movies, no one snaps their finger and suddenly transforms into Spiderman. It takes a willingness to fail multiple times to learn a new skill, whether that's getting better at socializing, or developing a talent. If a baby stopped trying to stand after the 10th or even 20th time of falling, she would never learn to walk. It's no different from anything else in life.

This next exercise will help you explore new skills or talents you'd like to develop, so you can begin to step outside of your comfort zone.

EXERCISE

Challenge Yourself to Grow

Get out a piece of paper and a pen and answer the following questions:

1. What quality do I admire the most in myself?
2. What do I do regularly to maintain or practice this quality?
3. What quality or skill would I like to develop further? Why?
4. If I developed this quality or skill, what would I be able to do that I don't feel like I can do now?

5. What is something I can do over the next month that would encourage me to grow in that direction?

When I was in high school, I was painfully shy and I was constantly second-guessing myself. I would mull over what I was about to say in my head five times before I actually said it. I even auditioned for a school play and choked on my words because I was nervous about being judged by the crowds. I was deeply uncomfortable in my own skin and wished for nothing more than to feel at ease with myself in front of other people.

Even though I desperately wanted to develop these skills, I never actually put in the effort *to* develop them. I spent more time trying to avoid social situations than I did trying to work on the part of myself that wanted to get better at them! I just hoped that someday my shyness would disappear.

Side note: I want to clarify that shyness is not bad or problematic. Some of the most successful and well-liked people are shy–they're even performers! It was an "issue" for me when it made it difficult for me to express myself effectively. I held back from making new friends and trying new things even though I wanted to because I was too self-conscious. I knew that being "shy" wasn't my authentic self because at home, I was loud and expressive (sometimes too expressive). In reality, I longed to share myself with the world but felt trapped in my own skin. Being "shy" for me was a mask.

So when doing this exercise, list things that don't go against your true nature. This exercise isn't about changing who you are as a person; it's about helping you unlock the authentic and best version of yourself, unrestricted by fear and self-doubt.

If I were to do the above exercise, my answers would have been like this.

What quality do I admire the most in myself?

I admire my ability to have compassion for other people and support them when they're feeling down.

What do I do regularly to maintain this quality?

I listen to people patiently. I offer emotional support when they need it. I also try to give good advice to my friends when they ask.

What is a quality that I would like to develop further? Why?

I'd like to be more outgoing and expressive around people, like how I am at home.

If I developed this quality, what would I be able to do that I don't feel like I can do now?

I'd be able to meet and interact with people without getting

nervous. I could have a much better time in all social environ-
ments, including class, school events, and friends' houses. I might
even try out for the school play. I'd be able to stand up in front of
the class and give presentations without feeling nervous and scared
and actually enjoy sharing my work with people.

What is something I can do over the next month that
would encourage me to grow in that direction?

I can start by volunteering to help at school events to meet more
people in a controlled environment. I can give a random person at
school a compliment during lunch. The next time we have presen-
tations, I can volunteer to go earlier than usual to challenge myself.
Maybe I can invite more people to hang out.

So think of something–whether it's a skill or a quality–that
you want to improve and you are actually motivated to do.
Then list a few action steps that will take you closer to your
goal (no matter how insignificant they may sound) and start
checking them off a list. By giving yourself small, immediate
challenges, you are signaling to your brain that you are open
to growth and new experiences.

In this process, remember that change doesn't happen
overnight. Be patient. Every time you step outside of your
comfort zone, you're evolving.

It wasn't until my mid-twenties, when I auditioned for film
and TV in Los Angeles, that I was forced to confront my fear

of performing in front of other people. It wasn't an easy process, and it probably took over 50 auditions before I felt "comfortable" in the audition room. When I started, I could barely deliver one line without my voice shaking. A casting director even told my manager that her pitch to get me into the room was better than I was. Ouch! Did it hurt? Yes. But a month later, I booked my first TV show. Why? Because I used that failure as fuel to push me forward.

People who try new things and put themselves out there *always* get rewarded in one way or another. The benefit may not come immediately, but I can't tell you how many times I've seen someone take a leap of faith and do something that sounded utterly ludicrous. Still, after years of focused effort, they eventually landed some success. The key was that they never gave up on themselves. Despite negativity and skepticism from others, they maintained their strong sense of self. And in the end, they were rewarded for it. Remember, your ability to succeed in life is almost always proportionate to your willingness to fail.

So step into the role as the main character in your life. See challenge as an opportunity to grow. Ask yourself: "What would the hero in me do in this situation?" When you open the door to possibility, you never know what's waiting for you.

Like Einstein once said, "Failure is success in progress."

11

CREATE HEALTHY HABITS

MIND, BODY, AND SOUL

“Health is a state of complete harmony of the body, mind and spirit.”

— *B.K.S. IYENGAR*

When you're rewiring your focus from the negative to the positive, creating new physical habits will help signal to your body that you are ready for change.

When I was in the beginning stages of my self-growth journey, I didn't feel like doing much of anything on a physical level. I was already adding so much mental and emotional work to my life that any extra effort felt draining. However, when I finally started incorporating some healthier habits into my routine, I found that the mental and emotional changes were easier to make because my physical energy was also shifting.

At first, I started with small changes in my lifestyle, like adding more fruit and vegetables to my day and going on weekly walks. After those became routine, I began to hike, journal, and spend more time in nature.

Let me be clear that this was a gradual evolution and did not happen all at once. So please don't set unrealistic expectations for yourself. Be patient and go slow. Below are some suggestions that will help you get started.

EXERCISES

10-Minute Jog

I've never liked jogging, and I still can't understand people who do (my husband). What I do know, however, is that every time I force myself on the treadmill or take a jog around the neighborhood, my body feels re-energized, and my mind feels clear and strong.

Research from Tsukuba University published in *Scientific Reports* has shown the benefits of taking short jogs. After just a 10-minute jog, participants in the study showed elevated moods and even performed better on the cognitive tasks. That's after 10 minutes of jogging!

The next time you're having brain fog and don't have enough energy to start your homework? Instead of downing an energy drink, take a short jog around the neighborhood and see how that fuels you for the rest of the day.

Small Food Shifts

There's an old saying that "you are what you eat." I always thought that was a bunch of nonsense until I actually felt how true that was in my body. As someone who used to live off cereal three meals a day, my entire life changed when I started to eat real food. I had more energy, lost some weight (naturally), and my skin cleared up.

Don't worry; I'm not suggesting that you overhaul your diet, and this definitely isn't about calorie counting. What I am suggesting is making minor additions and substitutions to your existing diet that can be easily implemented.

What are some easy substitutions you can make? If you like to eat desserts, maybe substitute that for a banana with peanut butter. Or, if you like to snack on chips, try replacing them with carrots and hummus. If you like eating energy bars, why not try salted nuts, instead?

A few other suggestions:

- Start your mornings with a glass of water.

- Add carrots to your afternoon snacks.
- Drink a sugar-free electrolyte mix with water, instead of energy drinks or soda.

Most of our diets simply don't provide all the nutrients we need, and sometimes vitamin deficiencies can manifest in bad moods, inability to concentrate, and sluggishness. As a teen who is still physically developing, it's even more important to be aware of your nutritional intake.

Vitamin supplements can also be a great way to make up for anything you might be lacking. For example, did you know that 42% of the US population is deficient in Vitamin D? However, it's one of the essential vitamins that has been shown to boost your mood, support your immune system, and build strong bones. Vitamin C is necessary for its collagen-building properties. Vitamin B12 and B6 are essential in maintaining proper energy levels, metabolizing fats, carbs, and proteins, and producing red blood cells.

Start with one minor diet adjustment and continue adding small changes. You'll see how much it will motivate you to keep improving!

Yoga

Yoga is a great practice to increase flexibility and build strength, but it's also been shown to be an effective alternative treatment to MDD or major depressive disorder. Other benefits include reduced anxiety, reduced inflammation, improved brain function, and increased self-esteem. Impressive, yes?

It's also so easy to do nowadays, so there are no excuses. Search online for "15-minute yoga exercises" or "20-minute yoga for stress reduction," and you'll find an endless selection of free videos.

Whenever you feel overwhelmed by life, I highly suggest incorporating a small yoga practice into your weekly routine. Even just 10 minutes a day can do wonders for your well-being.

Positive Media Consumption

Just like the phrase "you are what you eat," this applies to our content, as well. I'm picky about the type of content I watch, read, and listen to because I know how it will impact the rest of my day.

If I spend more time listening to inspiring podcasts and watching educational content, I'm much more likely to feel motivated, inspired, and optimistic about myself and the world around me. When I spend more time watching content with hate and negativity, I know I'm more prone to tuning into *those* feelings throughout the day.

We spend so much time on our devices, we have to be extra picky about where we plug ourselves into. Instead of mindlessly scrolling through your social media feeds, I highly suggest investing in content that uplifts your mood and elevates your sense of self—for example, motivational speakers, TED Talks, tutorials, or books geared toward self-improvement.

Get Creative

We're all guilty of turning to our phones when we're suffering from boredom. Still, if you're 100% honest, you probably find that consuming social media for extended periods is just energy draining. How often do you come away from a two-hour phone session thinking, *"that was time well spent!"*

Like meditation, doing something creative with your hands is one of the best ways to reset your mind and restore mental and emotional wellness.

Psychological studies have shown that crafts can help people reach the "steady-flow" state where all worries and stress dissipates as you focus intently on a single activity.

So think of an activity you do with your hands that appeals to you. This can be journaling, painting your room, sketching, writing stories, gardening, sewing–anything that requires your focused attention and switches on your creative brain! You'll be surprised by just how addicting it can be.

Self-Appreciation

Can you love and appreciate yourself right now? Whenever you need a pick-me-up or are slipping into self-doubt, give yourself full permission to love yourself for where you are in this moment.

Get out a pen and paper and write down five things you love about yourself. It might look something like this:

I love myself no matter what because…

1. I am a great friend.
2. I work hard for the things I care about.
3. I am a kind person.
4. I am dedicated to my growth every day.
5. I am resilient.

Repeat these back to yourself, and let these words sink into your body. We are often so quick to criticize ourselves for not being "perfect," yet, we rarely appreciate the things we *do* have going on! It's time to give yourself some credit for the amazing person you are.

AFTERWORD

The teenage years are some of our most confusing and frustrating years. Not only do we have the pressures of tests and homework, but throw in peer pressure and hormones, and we have a recipe for emotional and psychological chaos. As someone who has gone through it, I can say that that was very true for me.

Now that you've reached the end of this book, you may be tempted to shelve it and never open or think about it again, but I *highly* encourage you to at least bookmark the pages with the exercises, or better yet, write a few of them down so that you can refer back to them when you're ready.

I also want to emphasize that there is no wrong or right way of doing these exercises. You can start with one or two exercises that resonate with you the most and go from there. The worst thing you can do is become so overwhelmed by all of the information that you don't do any of them! Remember, there is no perfect way of going about your hero's journey. It's just important that you start.

There will be times in your life when you'll feel discouraged and want to throw in the towel and wallow. I hope in those moments you can be gentle with yourself. I hope you can give yourself the compassion and patience that you deserve. And ultimately, I hope you summon the courage to move on. I can illuminate the way, but you have to walk the path.

A friend once told me that as a young child, his father said that he would never amount to anything in life. My friend had two options–to believe his father or make a conscious decision to determine his own fate. Today, he's a very successful man who inspires thousands of people to be their best selves.

If you take one thing away from this book, it's this: you and only you define your value, path, and destiny. No one else. Not your parents, your friends, your teachers, or your school. Not even a job, money, house, or car can do that. You can either see that as discouraging or incredibly empowering. That's all up to you.

If I had succumbed to the negative opinions of the people around me or held onto the limiting beliefs that I developed in childhood, I would have never had the ability to do half of the things I've done and will continue to do in my life. I would have never written this book so that I could tell you that you can do the same.

My genuine hope is that you are beginning to see that there is a way you can interact with the world that is positive, empowering, and even exciting. That whenever you encounter a challenge in life, you can see it as an opportunity to grow. That you build such a strong sense of self, no one can deny your value. And most importantly, you love yourself so deeply that you dare to see every stumble as just one more step toward success.

If our lives result from how we choose to see ourselves and the world around us, I ask you this: How do you want to experience life? How do you want to see yourself?

I hope you choose radiant, brilliant, and fabulous. Remember, as the hero of your life you deserve no less.

PLEASE LEAVE A REVIEW

If you enjoyed this book and found value,
please consider leaving us a review so that others may
benefit from the tools.

Thank you.

BIBLIOGRAPHY

"Anxiety in Teens Is Rising: What's Going on?" *HealthyChildren.org*, https://www.healthychildren.org/English/health-issues/conditions/emotional-problems/Pages/Anxiety-Disorders.aspx.

Kidshelpline101, director. *YouTube*, YouTube, 1 June 2021, https://www.youtube.com/watch?v=eD1wliuHxHI. Accessed 19 Aug. 2022.

"What Does It Mean to Have a Strong Sense of Self? 6 Signs to Look For." *Mindbodygreen*, https://www.mindbodygreen.com/articles/how-to-develop-your-sense-of-self/.

Anthony, Kiara. "What Is EFT Tapping? 5-Step Technique for Anxiety Relief." *Healthline*, Healthline Media, 18 Sept. 2018, https://www.healthline.com/health/eft-tapping.

"The Tapping Solution Documentary." *YouTube*, https://youtu.be/9UypGSQtzFw. Accessed 19 Aug. 2022.

Scharping, Nathaniel. "Can Breathing Like Wim Hof Make Us Superhuman?" *Discover Magazine*, Discover Magazine, 17 Apr. 2020, https://www.discovermagazine.com/health/can-breathing-like-wim-hof-make-us-superhuman.

Moore, John. "5 Mental Exercises to Rewire Your Brain to Be More Positive." *Everyday Power*, 8 July 2022, https://everydaypower.com/mental-exercises-be-more-positive/.

Rice, Andrea. "Rewiring Your Brain for Positivity." *Psych Central*, Psych Central, 23 Nov. 2021, https://psychcentral.com/health/rewiring-your-brain-for-positivity-with-gratitude.

Reflections, Margaret's. "How to Use Your Imagination to Improve Your Performance." *Medium*, Better Humans, 4 Apr. 2022, https://betterhumans.pub/how-to-use-your-imagination-to-improve-your-performance-b96d4fdd7e37.

Lewis, Niamh. "How Amputee Jacky Hunt-Broersma Ran 104 Marathons in 104 Days: 'Just Focus on the next Step'." *ESPN*, ESPN Internet Ventures, 5 May 2022, https://www.espn.com/espn/story/_/id/33859427/how-amputee-jacky-hunt-broersma-ran-104-marathons-104-days-just-focus-next-step.

"Cornel Hrisca-Munn an All-Round Inspirational Person and Musician." *The Music Man*, 26 Aug. 2020, https://www.themusicman.uk/cornel-hrisca-munn/.

Monet, et al. "10 Incredible Blind Painters." *Everyday Sight*, 23 June 2019, https://www.everydaysight.com/blind-painters/.

Anderer, John. "Two Major Benefits of Running Just 10 Minutes a Day, New Study Says." *Eat This Not That*, 9 Dec. 2021, https://www.eatthis.-com/news-running-mood-study/.

Shah, Anjali. "Best Vitamins for Teens (2022 Guide)." *The Picky Eater*, 25 Feb. 2022, https://pickyeaterblog.com/best-vitamins-for-teens/.

About Stephanie Wheeler Stephanie Wheeler is the Director of Wellness at Mercy Medical Center. She holds a master's degree in exercise physiology and has worked in cardiac rehab and general fitness since 1998. Certified by the American College of Spo, et al. "42% Of Americans Are Vitamin D Deficient. Are You among Them?" *Mercy Medical Center*, 21 Nov. 2018, https://www.cantonmercy.org/healthchat/42-percent-of-americans-are-vitamin-d-deficient/#:~:text=Unfortunate-ly%2C%20about%2042%25%20of%20the,take%20prescription%20medica-tion%20long%20term.

Printed in Great Britain
by Amazon

24351552R00084